TOP NOTCH 1

D0163770

Workbook

Joan Saslow ■ Allen Ascher

with Barbara R. Denman

PEARSON
Longman

Top Notch: English for Today's World 1
Workbook

Pearson Education, 10 Bank Street, White Plains, NY 10606

Editorial director: Pamela Fishman
Senior development editor: Peter Benson
Assistant editor: Siobhan Sullivan
Vice president, director of design and production: Rhea Banker
Director of electronic production: Aliza Greenblatt
Managing editor: Mike Kemper
Art director: Ann France
Senior manufacturing buyer: Dave Dickey
Photo research: Aerin Csigay
Text composition: Word & Image Design Studio, Inc.
Full-service production provided by Camelot Editorial Services
Text font: Frutiger 10/12
Cover Photograph: "From Above," by Rhea Banker. Copyright © 2005 Rhea Banker.

ISBN: 0-13-110416-0

Photo credits:

Page 1: Reuters/Corbis; page 7: Ross Kinnaird/Getty Images; page 11: (left) Frank Micelotta/Getty Images, (middle left) Jason Fulford, photo courtesy of American International Artists, (middle right) Tim Mosenfelder/Corbis, (right) Hulton-Deutsch Collection/Corbis; page 16: Randy Taylor/Index Stock Imagery; page 19: Michal Heron; page 20: (Mary and Mark) Ryan McVay/Getty Images, (Jane) Cleve Bryant/PhotoEdit, (Rita, Evan, Bill, & Kim) Royalty Free/Corbis; page 24: (top) Myrleen Ferguson Cate/PhotoEdit, (bottom) Jerome Tisne/Getty Images; page 26: Nathaniel S. Butler/NBAE/Getty Images; page 36: Dorling Kindersley Media Library; page 38: (microwave) Anthony Meshkinyar/Getty Images, (PDA) Ryan McVay/Getty Images, (CD burner) Iomega Corporation, (hair dryer) Silver Burdett Ginn, (photocopier) Getty Images, (printer) Epson America, Inc., (cell phone) Nokia; page 49: Richard T. Nowitz/Corbis; page 54: Michal Heron; page 59: Michal Heron; page 60: (hair dryer) Silver Burdett Ginn, (photocopier) Getty Images; page 61: (grandparents) Lindy Powers/Index Stock Imagery, (children; boots) Michal Heron; page 64: (left) Jess Stock/Getty Images, (middle left) Dorling Kindersley Media Library, (middle right) Thomas Craig/Index Stock Imagery, (right) Robert Holmes/Corbis; page 67: Ron Chapple/Getty Images; page 69: Phil Cantor/Index Stock Imagery; page 71: Bill Bachmann/ Index Stock Imagery; page 73: Royalty-Free/Corbis; (bottom) LWA-Dann Tardif/Corbis; (right) James Marshall/Corbis; page 78: Steve Vidler/ eStock Photography LLC; page 79: Michal Heron; page 88: Michal Heron, (right) Courtesy of West Edmonton Mall.

Illustration credits:

Steve Attoe: pages 10, 17, 35, 58 (bottom), 76; Kenneth Batelman: pages 60, 61, 64; Pierre Berthiaume: page 82; Richard Burlew: page 49; Leanne Franson: pages 3, 31, 62, 68; Scott Fray: pages 60, 61; Steve Gardner: page 90; Brian Hughes: pages 13, 87; Stephen Hutchings: pages 5, 14, 40, 42, 44; André Labrie: page 72; Andy Meyer: pages 81, 82; Suzanne Mogensen: pages 29, 80, 85; Dusan Petričic: pages 21, 39 (bottom), 60, 83; Michel Rabagliati: pages 25, 63; Robert Saunders: page 22; NSV Productions: pages 30, 33, 39, 41, 58 (top), 86, 87.

Printed in the United States of America
17–V004–11 10 09

CONTENTS

Getting Acquainted

TOPIC PREVIEW

1 ▶ Read about the famous person. Then check ☑ <u>true</u>, <u>false</u>, or <u>no information</u> according to the website.

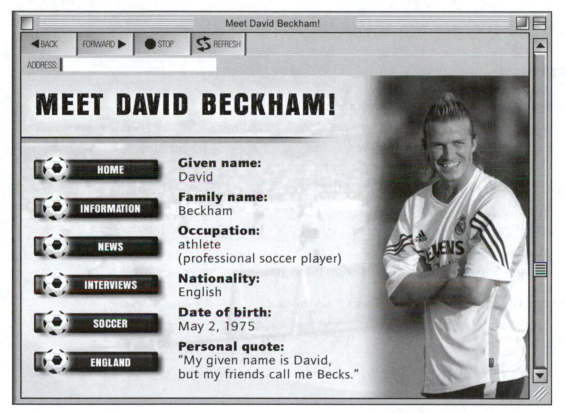

SOURCE: <u>www.beckham-magazine.com</u>

	true	false	no information
1. His first name is David.	☐	☐	☐
2. His last name is Becks.	☐	☐	☐
3. He is an actor.	☐	☐	☐
4. He is married.	☐	☐	☐
5. His friends call him David.	☐	☐	☐

2 ▶ Match the word or words with the same meaning. Draw a line.

1. Nice to meet you.　　　　**a.** not married

2. first name　　　　**b.** given name

3. last name　　　　**c.** Good to meet you.

4. single　　　　**d.** family name

3 ▸ WHAT ABOUT YOU? Complete the information. Write <u>your</u> name on the lines.

> ### HELLO
>
> MY NAME IS _____.
>   first name   last name
>
> PLEASE CALL ME _____.

LESSON 1

4 ▸ **Choose the correct response. Circle the letter.**

1. "It's a pleasure to meet you, Choi."
   a. Good.   **b.** Yes, I am.   **c.** You, too.

2. "Are you new here?"
   a. Yes, we are.   **b.** Yes, they are.   **c.** Yes, he is.

3. "Is Mr. Adams married?"
   a. No, she isn't.   **b.** No, he isn't.   **c.** Yes, they are.

4. "Are you John?"
   a. That's Sam over there.   **b.** Nice to meet you, John.   **c.** As a matter of fact, I am.

5 ▸ **Complete the conversations. Use words from the box.**

meet	over	think	too	that	am	is

1. **A:** Are you a student here?

   B: Yes, I _____. I'm Tanja.

   A: I'm Claudio. It's nice to _____ you, Tanja.

   B: You, _____, Claudio.

2. **A:** Is _____ the new manager _____ there?

   B: Yes. That's Ms. Douglas. She's from New Zealand.

   A: _____ she from Wellington?

   B: No, she isn't. I _____ she's from Auckland.

6 ▸ **Look at the responses. Complete the <u>yes</u> / <u>no</u> questions with <u>be</u>.**

1. **A:** <u>*Are you*</u> Stacey?
   B: No, I'm not. I'm Claire.

2. **A:** _____ English?
   B: No, they're not. They're Australian.

3. **A:** _____ a student here?
   B: Yes, she is. She's new.

4. **A:** _____ married?
   B: No, he's not. He's single.

5. **A:** _____ in our class?
   B: Yes, we are.

6. **A:** _____ an art teacher?
   B: Yes, as a matter of fact, I am.

7 Look at the pictures. Write short answers about the people.

We're students.

I'm a soccer player.

Andy and Tara

John

1. Are Andy and Tara students?

   _Yes, they are_____.

2. Is John an athlete?

   _____.

I'm from Mexico.

MEXICO

This is my wife, Linda.

Maria

Linda and Mike

3. Is Maria from Venezuela?

   _____.

4. Are Linda and Mike married?

   _____.

8 CHALLENGE. Write <u>yes</u> / <u>no</u> questions and give short answers. Use contractions when possible.

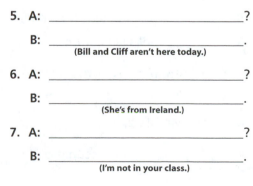

1. **A:** _Are you Paul_____?

   B: _No, I'm not_____.
   (I am not Paul.)

2. **A:** _Are they the new teachers_?

   B: _Yes, they are_____.
   (They are the new teachers.)

3. **A:** _____?

   B: _____.
   (He's not married.)

4. **A:** _____?

   B: _____.
   (We're from Kyoto.)

5. **A:** _____?

   B: _____.
   (Bill and Cliff aren't here today.)

6. **A:** _____?

   B: _____.
   (She's from Ireland.)

7. **A:** _____?

   B: _____.
   (I'm not in your class.)

9 ▷ **WHAT ABOUT YOU?** Answer the questions. Use your <u>own</u> words.

1. "Are you a new student?" (YOU) _____.

2. "Are you an athlete?" (YOU) _____.

3. "Are you married?" (YOU) _____.

LESSON 2

10 ▷ Complete the conversations. Use words from the box.

they	their	you	your	he	his	she	her	we	our

1. **A:** Who's that?

   B: That's Ajit's brother. _____ name is Rajeev, but everyone calls him Raj.

   A: How old is _____?

   B: Twenty-three, I think.

2. **A:** Are _____ the new English teacher?

   B: Yes, I am.

   A: Hi, I'm Steve. What's _____ name?

   B: Doug Stearns. But everyone calls me DJ.

3. **A:** These are my two sons.

   B: What are _____ names?

   A: Todd and Allen.

   B: Are _____ students?

   A: Yes, they are.

4. **A:** Hi, Ha-na.

   B: Hello, Su-ji. Are _____ classmates again?

   A: Yes, I think so. Is that _____ teacher over there?

   B: Yes. _____ name is Mrs. Kim.

   A: _____ looks very young!

Most Common Family Names

Country	Family Name
China	Li
France	Martin
Great Britain	Smith
India	Patel
Japan	Sato
Korea	Kim
Russia	Ivanov
Spain	Garcia
United States	Smith
Vietnam	Nguyen

11 ▷ Complete the information questions. Use contractions when possible.

1. **A:** _Who's_____ that?
   B: That's Mr. Matz.

2. **A:** _____ his occupation?
   B: He's an artist.

3. **A:** Your daughter is very cute.
   _____ she?
   B: She's eight months old.

4. **A:** I'll send you an e-mail.
   _____ your e-mail address?
   B: It's une-yoshiko@videotech.co.jp.

5. **A:** _____ Anil and Temel from?
   B: They're from Istanbul, I think.

6. **A:** _____ your new classmates?
   B: That's Marcos on the right and Paulo on the left.

12 Choose the correct response. Write the letter on the line.

1. ____ "How old is Michael?"
2. ____ "Who's not here?"
3. ____ "What are your occupations?"
4. ____ "Where are their friends from?"
5. ____ "Where is Diana?"
6. ____ "What's that?"
7. ____ "Who are your teachers?"

a. She's over there.
b. They're from Germany.
c. He's three.
d. Rachel isn't here.
e. Their names are Mr. Park and Ms. Kim.
f. I'm a singer, and he's a student.
g. That's a student information form.

13 Look at the picture. Write a question for each answer.

1. A: _____?

   B: They're my friends from computer class.

2. A: _____?

   B: Their names are Juan and Paloma.

3. A: _____?

   B: Spain.

4. A: _____?

   B: She's two years old.

14 WHAT ABOUT YOU? Answer the questions. Use your <u>own</u> words.

1. "What's your occupation?" YOU _____.

2. "Who's under 15 years old in your family?" YOU _____.

3. "What's your mother's name?" YOU _____.

4. "How old are you?" YOU _____.

15 Read the letter and reply on an intercultural exchange website.

Ask Allen
Advice for International Travelers

Intercultural Exchange.com

Favorites

History

Search

What's in a first name? In many countries, it's the last.

Dear Allen,

I have a problem. My name is Chinese. It's Zhang Yin. Zhang is my last name and Yin is my first name. In China, family names are first and given names are last. I'm a salesman and I often travel to English-speaking countries for business. When I fill out a personal information form in English, I write <u>Yin</u> in the box for first name and <u>Zhang</u> in the box for last name. Then people call me Yin Zhang. When I introduce myself as Zhang Yin, they call me Mr. Yin. So sometimes I say that my name is Yin Zhang. But I don't feel comfortable with that because that isn't my real name. What should I do?

Zhang Yin
Shanghai, China

Dear Yin,

In English-speaking countries, when you ask, "What's your name?" you always get the person's given name first and the family name last. In China, and in many Asian countries, including Japan and Korea, the family name is first and given name is second. To avoid confusion, try introducing yourself like this: "Hi. I'm Zhang Yin. My first name is Yin and my family name is Zhang. Please call me Mr. Zhang."

Allen

Now read the sentences. Check ✔ <u>true</u>, <u>false</u>, or <u>no information</u>.

	true	false	no information
1. Zhang Yin's family name is Yin.	☐	☐	☐
2. Zhang Yin is a pilot.	☐	☐	☐
3. In China, you say a person's family name first and given name last.	☐	☐	☐
4. Zhang Yin is from China.	☐	☐	☐
5. Zhang Yin is married.	☐	☐	☐

16 WHAT ABOUT YOU? Answer the questions. Use your <u>own</u> words.

1. "In this country, are family names first or are given names first?"

   (YOU) _____.

2. "What's your nickname?"

   (YOU) _____.

3. "What do you call your teacher?"

   (YOU) _____.

17 Read the questions. Who is it OK to say this to? Check ✔ <u>OK</u> or <u>Not OK</u>.

Question	Person to ask	OK	Not OK
1. What's your first name?	your friend's friend	☐	☐
2. Are you married?	your manager	☐	☐
3. How old are you?	your teacher	☐	☐
4. What do you do?	your father's friend	☐	☐
5. What's your nickname?	your friend's grandfather	☐	☐
6. Where are you from?	your classmate	☐	☐

18 Read about a famous athlete.

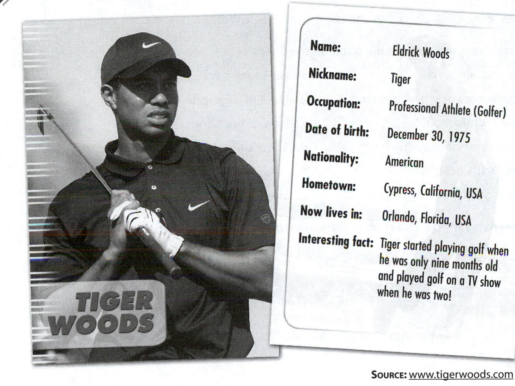

Name:	Eldrick Woods
Nickname:	Tiger
Occupation:	Professional Athlete (Golfer)
Date of birth:	December 30, 1975
Nationality:	American
Hometown:	Cypress, California, USA
Now lives in:	Orlando, Florida, USA
Interesting fact:	Tiger started playing golf when he was only nine months old and played golf on a TV show when he was two!

SOURCE: www.tigerwoods.com

Now write a short biography of Mr. Woods. Use the biographies on page 13 in the Student's Book as a model.

GRAMMAR BOOSTER

A Choose the correct response. Circle the letter.

1. "Are you from Italy?"
   a. Yes, I am. **b.** No, he's not. **c.** Yes, they are.

2. "Is she late?"
   a. No, she is. **b.** Yes, we are. **c.** Yes, she is.

3. "Are they teachers?"
   a. No, I'm not. **b.** Yes, they are. **c.** No, she isn't.

4. "Is Canada a language?"
   a. Yes, she is. **b.** No, it isn't. **c.** Yes, it is.

5. "Is Jim married?"
   a. Yes, they are. **b.** Yes, he is. **c.** Yes, I am.

B Choose the correct response. Write the letter on the line.

1. _____ "Are you a musician?"   **a.** His name's Ivan.

2. _____ "Where are your parents from?"   **b.** No, I'm a graphic designer.

3. _____ "How old are you?"   **c.** He's a manager.

4. _____ "What's her nationality?"   **d.** São Paulo. But they live in Santos now.

5. _____ "What's his occupation?"   **e.** Twenty.

6. _____ "Who's your friend?"   **f.** She's Australian.

C Complete the conversations. Use contractions when possible.

1. **A:** Is she Chinese?
   B: No, _she's_____ Russian.

2. **A:** Who's that?
   B: _____ my teacher. His name is Mr. Hopkins.

3. **A:** What's their last name?
   B: _____ Johnson.

4. **A:** How old is your brother?
   B: _____ twenty-three.

5. **A:** Where's London?
   B: _____ in England.

6. **A:** What are your children's names?
   B: _____ Daniel and Susana.

7. **A:** Am I late for class?
   B: No, _____ late.

8. **A:** Are you a flight attendant?
   B: No, _____ a pilot.

D Complete the sentences with a possessive adjective from the box.

my	your	his	her	our	their

1. Cindy and Lee are new students. _____ teacher is Mr. Michaels.

2. Mr. Vidal is a computer programmer. _____ family lives in Paris.

3. Mrs. Ichikawa is from Tokyo. _____ nationality is Japanese.

4. Are you a chef? _____ chicken is very good.

5. I have two sisters. _____ sister Sarah lives in London and _____ sister Ellen lives in Brighton.

6. Sally and I are in a computer class. _____ class is at 9 a.m.

E Look at the responses. Write information questions. Use contractions when possible.

1. **A:** _How old is your son_ _____?

   B: My son? He's sixteen.

2. **A:** _____?

   B: My teacher's name is Linda Thomas.

3. **A:** _____?

   B: I'm from Turkey.

4. **A:** _____?

   B: They're students.

5. **A:** _____?

   B: It's Margaret. But my nickname is Meg.

6. **A:** _____?

   B: My address? It's 1932 West Street.

1 **Find the words in the puzzle. Circle each word. Words can be across (→) or down (↓).**

manager

salesperson

teacher

interpreter

programmer

photographer

designer

pilot

musician

chef

p	m	a	n	a	g	e	r	z	g	h	p	l
d	g	p	d	z	f	c	h	m	l	w	v	d
e	x	i	v	y	d	h	d	u	j	q	t	k
s	a	l	e	s	p	e	r	s	o	n	e	z
i	c	o	z	i	p	f	w	i	g	c	a	a
g	u	t	d	y	k	e	b	c	h	d	c	g
n	i	o	q	l	u	r	h	i	t	y	h	m
e	p	h	o	t	o	g	r	a	p	h	e	r
r	n	d	v	t	c	p	t	n	r	k	r	w
p	r	o	g	r	a	m	m	e	r	w	s	z
f	i	n	t	e	r	p	r	e	t	e	r	y

2 **Find the nationality. Unscramble the letters.**

1. Maxecni   = _____

2. Ciananad   = _____

3. Tishruk   = _____

4. Antigreenan   = _____

5. Banliziar   = _____

6. Lanseebe   = _____

A JOKE FOR YOU!

Her name is Pat, but we call her Patricia Anna Marie.

Going out

TOPIC PREVIEW

1 Look at the newspaper concert listings. Then complete the chart.

Who is playing?	What kind of music?	Where is it?	What time is the show?	How much are tickets?
Marc Anthony	Latin		10:30 p.m.	
James Carter		Riverfront Park		
				$15
	classical	City Music Hall		

2 **WHAT ABOUT YOU?** What's your style? Check ✔ **Not for me** or **More my style**.

Kind of concert	Not for me	More my style
an afternoon jazz concert in the park	☐	☐
a late night rock concert at a rock club	☐	☐
a Latin music concert at a dance club	☐	☐
a classical concert at a concert hall	☐	☐

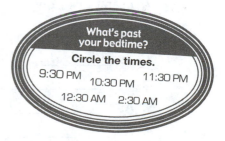

What's past your bedtime?
Circle the times.
9:30 PM   10:30 PM   11:30 PM
12:30 AM   2:30 AM

Jueves

3 WHAT ABOUT YOU? **Complete the paragraph with kinds of music and concert times. Use your <u>own</u> words.**

> I like _____ music, but _____ music isn't really my style. A concert at _____ is too late, but a concert at _____ is perfect for me.

LESSON 1

4 **Choose the correct response. Circle the letter.**

1. "What time's the show?"
   a. At the theater.　　　b. On Tuesday.　　　c. At 8:30.

2. "I'm busy on Saturday. What about Friday?"
   a. I'm not really a fan.　　b. Perfect.　　c. Too bad.

3. "Where's the concert?"
   a. Really? I'd love to go.　b. In the park.　　c. At noon.

4. "Do you want to see an art exhibit on Sunday?"
   a. I'd love to.　　　b. That's past my bedtime.　　c. On Monday.

5 **Put the conversation in order. Write the number on the line.**

_1_ Are you busy on Saturday night?

___ 10:00 p.m.? Well, I'd like to go, but that's past my bedtime.

___ Really? Sounds great! What time's the play?

___ *A Comedy of Errors* is at the Community Theater.

___ At 10:00 p.m. It's a late show.

___ No, I'm not. Why?

_7_ Too bad. Maybe some other time.

6 **Complete the sentences with <u>on</u>, <u>in</u>, or <u>at</u>.**

1. The movie theater is _____ Dewey Street.

2. Ana isn't here. She's _____ New York.

3. My music class is _____ the New City Music School. It's _____ the corner of Main and Park.

4. The talk is _____ 11:00 _____ the morning.

5. The play is _____ noon, _____ the park.

6. The Marc Anthony concert is _____ Friday, January 18th.

7. I can't talk right now. I'm _____ work. I'll call you when I get home.

7 **Write questions with <u>When</u>, <u>Where</u>, or <u>What time</u>. Use contractions when possible.**

1. A: *When's the play* _____? B: The play is on Wednesday.

2. A: _____? B: The concert is at 7:00.

3. A: _____? B: The school is on Newton Street.

4. A: _____? B: Tim's at work.

5. **A:** _____? **B:** His class is on Monday morning.

6. **A:** _____? **B:** The concert is in the park.

7. **A:** _____? **B:** My class is at 10:30.

8 ▷ **WHAT ABOUT YOU?** Answer the questions. Use your <u>own</u> words. Use <u>in</u>, <u>on</u>, or <u>at</u>.

1. "Where is your school?" (YOU) _____.

2. "What time is your English class?" (YOU) _____.

3. "When are you free this week?" (YOU) _____.

LESSON 2

9 ▷ Choose the correct responses to complete the conversation. Write the letter on the line.

A: Excuse me. I'm looking for Gino's Café.

B: _____
       1.

A: Yes. Is it around here?

B: _____
       2.

A: It's 610 Pine Street.

B: _____
       3.

A: Really? That's great. Thanks.

B: _____
       4.

a. Well, Pine Street is right around the corner.

b. I think it is. Do you know the address?

c. No problem.

d. Gino's? The Italian Café?

10 ▷ Look at the pictures. Write the locations on the line. Use words from the box.

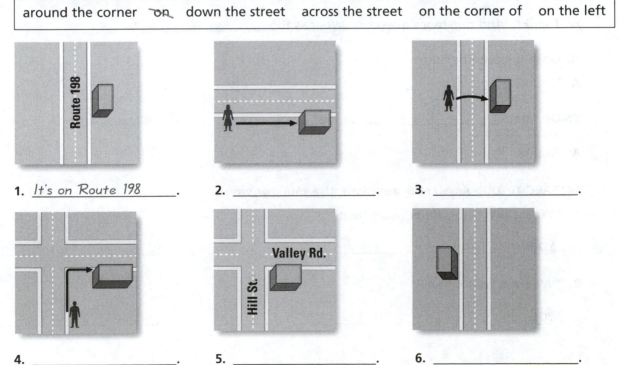

around the corner   ~~on~~   down the street   across the street   on the corner of   on the left

1. _It's on Route 198_ .

2. _____ .

3. _____ .

4. _____ .

5. _____ .

6. _____ .

11 ▷ CHALLENGE. Complete the conversation. Use the map and your <u>own</u> words.

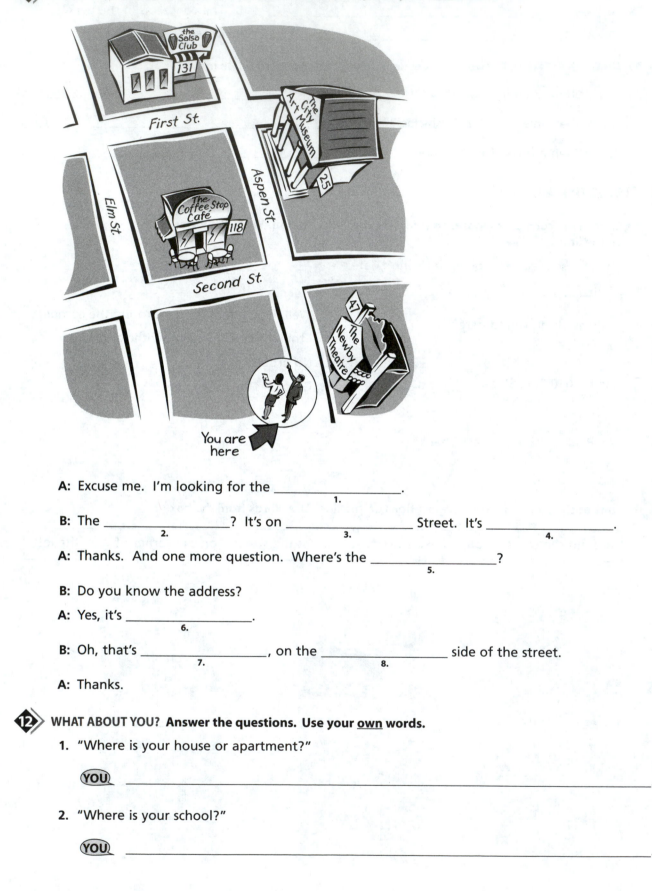

A: Excuse me. I'm looking for the _____.

                                             1.

B: The _____? It's on _____ Street. It's _____.

                     2.   **3.**   **4.**

A: Thanks. And one more question. Where's the _____?

                                                       5.

B: Do you know the address?

A: Yes, it's _____.

                   6.

B: Oh, that's _____, on the _____ side of the street.

                     7.   **8.**

A: Thanks.

12 ▷ WHAT ABOUT YOU? Answer the questions. Use your <u>own</u> words.

1. "Where is your house or apartment?"

    (YOU) _____.

2. "Where is your school?"

    (YOU) _____.

LESSONS 3 AND 4

13 Look at the festival events listing. Then answer the questions. Use <u>in</u>, <u>on</u>, or <u>at</u>, if possible.

10th Annual Asian Folk Festival

Events Listing

Saturday, May 10 at the Park Arts Center in Rand Park

	Time	Location	Event	
	1:00 PM	Rand Park	Kite-Making Workshop	Children can make their own kite to fly in the park
	3:00 PM	The Park Arts Theater	Japanese Play: Children's Kabuki Group	Watch middle school students from Kobe, Japan perform a traditional play
	7:00 PM	The Rand Park Band Shell	Javanese Concert: Kiai Kanjeng Gamelan Orchestra	Hear music featuring drums, cymbals, and gongs from Java, Indonesia
	6:00 PM	The Rand Park Band Shell	Korean Dance: "Bu-che Chum" Fan Dance Troupe	See colorful dancers from Suwon, Korea perform a beautiful fan dance
	5:00 PM and 9:45 PM	The Park Arts Theater	Chinese Movie: *The Story of Lotus*	A love story set in the beautiful Wuyi mountains in Southern China

Plus try traditional Asian treats from China, Japan, Korea, and Indonesia. Food stalls will be open in the park from 12:00 to 8:00 PM.

1. When's the Asian Folk Festival? _____.

2. Where's the Japanese play? _____.

3. What time is the Javanese concert? _____.

4. Where's the Chinese movie? _____.

5. What event is at 6:00 p.m.? _____.

14 Complete the instant messages with information from the Asian Folk Festival listing.

Lara - Conversation

File Edit Actions Tools Help

Invite   Send Files   Webcam   Audio   Launch Site

To: Lara Lara@email.com

Peter says: Hi, Lara. Are you free on [_____] ?
Lara says: Yes. Why? _1._
Peter says: The Asian Folk Festival is at the [_____] , in [_____] .
Lara says: What kind of festival? _2._ _3._
Peter says: An Asian culture festival. Let's see . . . There's a Chinese movie, a Japanese [_____] ,
  a Korean [_____] , and a Javanese [_____] . _4._
  _5._ _6._
Lara says: Really? Sounds like fun! 😊
Peter says: I know you're a movie fan. Want to see the movie?
Lara says: OK. 👍 What time?
Peter says: There's an early show at [_____] and a late show at 9:45.
  _7._

Lara says: Let's go to the early show—9:45 is past my bedtime! 😴

15 Read about the WOMAD festival. Then check ✔ <u>true</u>, <u>false</u>, or <u>no information</u>.

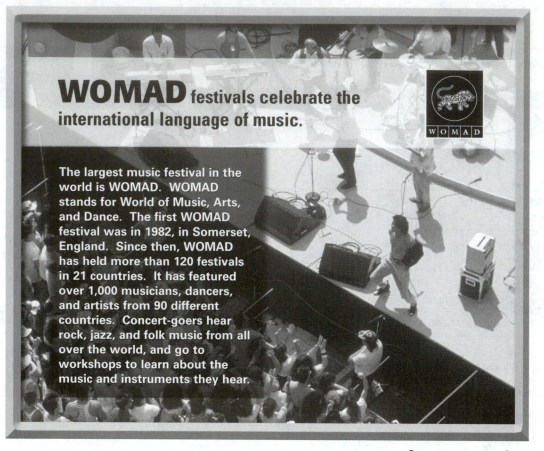

WOMAD festivals celebrate the international language of music.

The largest music festival in the world is WOMAD. WOMAD stands for World of Music, Arts, and Dance. The first WOMAD festival was in 1982, in Somerset, England. Since then, WOMAD has held more than 120 festivals in 21 countries. It has featured over 1,000 musicians, dancers, and artists from 90 different countries. Concert-goers hear rock, jazz, and folk music from all over the world, and go to workshops to learn about the music and instruments they hear.

SOURCE: www.womad.org

	true	false	no information
1. You can see a concert at the WOMAD festival.	☐	☐	☐
2. WOMAD is a classical music festival.	☐	☐	☐
3. WOMAD tickets cost $90.	☐	☐	☐
4. The musicians at WOMAD are from England.	☐	☐	☐

16 Write a short message to a friend. Invite your friend to an event. Use the Asian Folk Festival listing or your <u>own</u> event.

GRAMMAR **BOOSTER**

A Complete the sentences. Write <u>in</u>, <u>on</u>, or <u>at</u> on the line.

1. There's a jazz concert _____ Tuesday.
2. The theater is _____ 10 Bank St.
3. My brother lives _____ Rome.
4. I finish work _____ 5:00.
5. I'm busy _____ the morning.
6. Germany is _____ Europe.
7. My house is _____ Carmel Road.
8. My parents married _____ 1970.

B Choose the correct answer. Circle the letter.

1. "Where's the play?"
   a. At The Grand Theater. b. At 7:30. c. In the evening.

2. "What time's the movie?"
   a. In March. b. Tomorrow. c. At 8:10.

3. "When's the concert?"
   a. On Tuesday. b. On Ninth Avenue. c. At my school.

4. "What time is class?"
   a. At night. b. At 6:30. c. At the bank.

5. "Where's his meeting?"
   a. On Tuesday. b. At noon. c. At 44 South Street.

6. "When's the art exhibit?"
   a. In November. b. In the center of town. c. At the City Museum.

7. "What time's the talk?"
   a. March 13. b. Today. c. At 1 p.m.

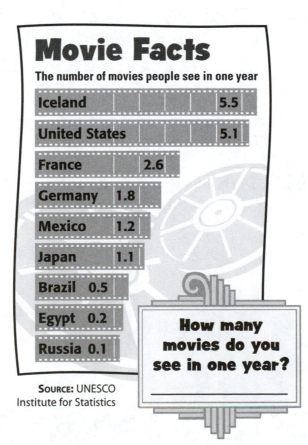

Movie Facts

The number of movies people see in one year

Iceland	5.5
United States	5.1
France	2.6
Germany	1.8
Mexico	1.2
Japan	1.1
Brazil	0.5
Egypt	0.2
Russia	0.1

SOURCE: UNESCO Institute for Statistics

How many movies do you see in one year?

_____

C Complete the event listings with prepositions of time and place. Write **in**, **at**, or **on**.

 # Arts Week
VOL 1.

Band Plans Free Concert

The Swingtime Jazz Band's first free concert is _at_ 8 PM ____
1.   2.
Monday. It's ____ Grand Hall ____ Wakefield Street ____ downtown
3.   4.   5.
Wellington. Call 999–555–8443 for more information.

Miracle Worker at Victoria University

Victoria University presents the play *The Miracle Worker* ____
6.
7:30 PM ____ Friday and Saturday, 4/23–4/24, and ____ 2:30 PM
7.   8.
____ April 25. The performances are ____ The Adam Concert Hall
9.   10.
____ Kelburn Road.
11.

D Complete the conversations. Write questions with **When**, **Where**, or **What**.
Complete the responses with a preposition.

1. **A:** _What time is the concert_ _____?

   B: I think the concert is _at_ 8:30.

2. **A:** _____?

   B: The play is ____ The Landry Theater.

3. **A:** _____?

   B: The supermarket is ____ Park Road.

4. **A:** _____?

   B: The exhibit is ____ January and February.

JUST FOR FUN

1 ▷ **Complete the crossword puzzle.**

Across

4. film

6. artists' show

8. performance with actors

Down

1. not busy

2. music performance

3. not left

5. the spelling of 30

7. not good

				1			
	2						3
4							
			5				
	6				7		
8							

A RIDDLE FOR YOU!

Question:
What's the number one musical instrument in the world?

Answer:
The human voice!

2 ▷ **BRAINTEASER. Who is a writer? A musician? An artist? An actor? Read the clues and complete the sentences.**

1. Ivan is an _____.

Clues:

Cleo's exhibit is at the City Gallery.

Paula is a rock guitarist with the group Jumbo.

Ivan is in a new play at the Cameo Theater.

Norman's talk is at Book World at 3:00.

2. Paula is a _____.

3. Cleo is an _____.

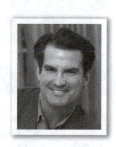

4. Norman is a _____.

Talking about Families

TOPIC PREVIEW

1 Complete the chart. Use words from the Student's Book.

Family Relationships		
Words for males	Words for females	Words for males or females
son	*daughter*	*children*

2 Complete the sentences with the correct family relationship.

1. My mother and my father are my _____.

2. My mother's father and my mother's mother are my _____.

3. My mother's brother's son is my _____.

4. My sister's _____ is my brother-in-law.

5. My brother's daughter is my _____.

6. My son and my daughter are my _____.

3 **CHALLENGE.** Look at the family tree website. Complete the sentences.

1. Rita is a _daughter-in-law_, a _wife_____, a _sister-in-law_, and a _mother_____.

2. Jane is a _____, a _____, a _____, and an _____.

3. Evan is a _____, a _____, a _____, and a _____.

4. Mark is a _____, a _____, a _____, and a _____.

Welcome to the Dalton Family Tree

You are visitor number:

1146

Mary   Mark

Bill   Rita

Kim   Evan

Jane

Thank you for visiting our web page. Please sign our guestbook!   CLICK HERE

LESSON 1

4 ▷ **Choose the correct response. Circle the letter.**

1. "Tell me about your family."
   a. Not really. **b.** Oh great! **c.** OK, sure.

2. "Who are those people?"
   a. They're married. **b.** They're my cousins. **c.** Yes, they are.

3. "Do you have a large family?"
   a. No, they don't. **b.** Yes, it does. **c.** No, I don't.

4. "Does he have any brothers or sisters?"
   a. No, he doesn't. **b.** He's an only child. **c.** No, he isn't.

5. "Do you look like your mother?"
   a. Yes, I do. **b.** No, she doesn't. **c.** Really?

5 ▷ **Complete the paragraph. Use words from the box.**

likes	doesn't like	works	has
live	work	doesn't have	lives

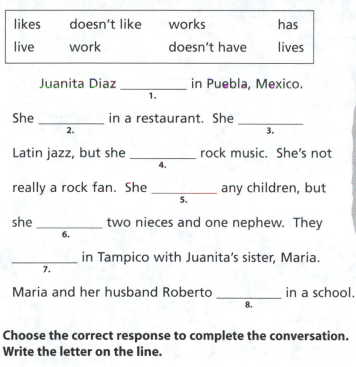

Juanita Diaz _____ in Puebla, Mexico.
                              1.

She _____ in a restaurant. She _____
        2.   **3.**

Latin jazz, but she _____ rock music. She's not
                              4.

really a rock fan. She _____ any children, but
                              5.

she _____ two nieces and one nephew. They
        6.

_____ in Tampico with Juanita's sister, Maria.
    7.

Maria and her husband Roberto _____ in a school.
                                        8.

6 ▷ **Choose the correct response to complete the conversation. Write the letter on the line.**

A: Do you like Australia?

B: _____
        1.

A: That's too bad. Tell me about your family.

B: _____
        2.

A: Do you have a large family?

B: _____
        3.

A: Is your brother married?

B: _____
        4.

A: Does he live near your parents?

B: _____
        5.

a. No, he's single.

b. Yes, he does.

c. OK. What would you like to know?

d. No, I don't. I have one brother, but I don't have any sisters.

e. Yes, I do, but my family isn't here.

7 Look at the birth rate chart. Check ✔ <u>true</u>, <u>false</u>, or <u>no information</u>.

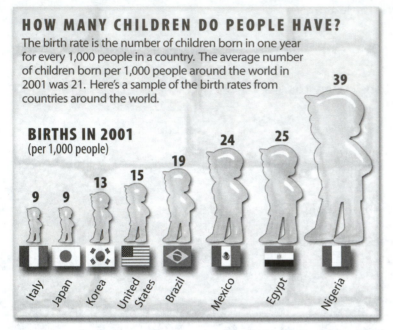

HOW MANY CHILDREN DO PEOPLE HAVE?

The birth rate is the number of children born in one year for every 1,000 people in a country. The average number of children born per 1,000 people around the world in 2001 was 21. Here's a sample of the birth rates from countries around the world.

BIRTHS IN 2001
(per 1,000 people)

Italy	Japan	Korea	United States	Brazil	Mexico	Egypt	Nigeria
9	9	13	15	19	24	25	39

Source: www.worldbank.org

	true	false	no information
1. The birth rate in Mexico is 24.	☐	☐	☐
2. The average family in Japan has 9 children.	☐	☐	☐
3. The average birth rate around the world is 39.	☐	☐	☐

8 Look at the pictures. Write sentences.

1. _They're married_ . 2. _____ . 3. _____ . 4. _____ .

9 How old are people when they get married? Look at the chart.

Age at first marriage					
Country	China	Peru	Sweden	Tunisia	United States
Men	23	25	34	30	28
Women	22	23	31	26	26

Source: United Nations Statistics Division

In these countries, are men or women older when they get married? _____ .

10 **Look at the responses. Write questions. Use words from each box.**

Do Does	+	your daughter you your brother the manager your parents	+	like have work speak look live	+	like you? French? on King Street? any photos of your family? on Saturdays? this music?

1. **A:** *Do your parents speak French* ? **B:** Yes, they do.
2. **A:** _____ ? **B:** No, he doesn't.
3. **A:** _____ ? **B:** Yes, I think I do.
4. **A:** _____ ? **B:** No, she doesn't.
5. **A:** _____ ? **B:** Yes, she does.

11 **WHAT ABOUT YOU? Answer the questions. Use your own words.**

1. "Do you speak English with your family?"

   (YOU) _____ .

2. "Does your family have a website?"

   (YOU) _____ .

3. "Do you live near your parents?"

   (YOU) _____ .

LESSON 2

12 **Complete the questions with do or does.**

1. Where _____ George live?

2. What _____ your sister-in-law do?

3. When _____ you listen to music?

4. What time _____ your son go to school?

5. What _____ your friends call you?

6. How many sisters _____ you have?

How many people are there in the world? You can see a population clock on this website:
www.census.gov/cgi-bin/ipc/popclockw

13 **Choose the correct response. Write the letter on the line.**

1. ____ "What does Alex do?"

2. ____ "How many grandchildren do you have?"

3. ____ "Where does your mother live?"

4. ____ "What time do you go home?"

5. ____ "When do you visit your grandmother?"

6. ____ "What do you and your husband do?"

a. She lives with my sister in Madrid.

b. At 6:30.

c. He works at a bookstore.

d. I see her every July and December.

e. I have three.

f. We're both teachers.

14 Look at the responses. Complete the questions.

1. A: _What does_ Luigi _do_ ?
   B: He's a computer programmer.

2. A: _____ your cousins _____?
   B: They live in Hong Kong.

3. A: _____ your mother
   _____ you?
   B: She visits me every year in May.

4. A: _____ concert tickets _____?
   B: I only have two.

5. A: _____ to school?
   B: We go at 8:30.

6. A: _____ your younger
   brother _____?
   B: He looks like me. He's really cute!

15 WHAT ABOUT YOU? Write a paragraph about someone in <u>your</u> family.
Use the questions for ideas.

• Where does he or she live and work?

• Who lives with him or her?

• What does he or she do?

• When do you see him or her?

LESSONS 3 AND 4

16 Read the article. Then answer the questions.

Multiple births happen when more than one baby is born to the same woman at the same time. Twins are an example of a multiple birth; so are triplets (three babies born at the same time), quadruplets (four babies), and quintuplets (five babies). How common are they? In Australia, twins are born in about 1 out of 80 births, and triplets in about 1 out of 6,400 births. In the United States, twins are born in about 1 out of 33 births. Triplets are born in about 1 out of 585 births. In 2001, 1 out of about 47,000 births was quintuplets—or more!

Twins usually have the same birthday. But some twins are born on different days. And in late December 1999, some twins were born in two different centuries— one twin in 1999, and one in the year 2000!

1. Where are twins born in about 1 out of 33 births? _____.

2. What do you call three babies born at the same time? _____.

3. Do all twins have the same birthday? _____.

17 Look at the pictures. Check ☑ all the sentences that are true.

1. ☐ **a.** Mary and Ida both wear glasses.
   ☐ **b.** Mary wears glasses, but Ida doesn't.
   ☐ **c.** Mary wears glasses, and Ida does too.

2. ☐ **a.** Miki is a chef, but Jamie isn't.
   ☐ **b.** Miki isn't a chef, and Jamie isn't either.
   ☐ **c.** Miki is a chef, and Jamie is too.

3. ☐ **a.** Antonio speaks English, and Yoko does too.
   ☐ **b.** Antonio and Yoko both speak English.
   ☐ **c.** Antonio speaks English, but Yoko doesn't.

4. ☐ **a.** Jim is a jazz fan, but Thomas isn't.
   ☐ **b.** Jim isn't a jazz fan, and Thomas isn't either.
   ☐ **c.** Jim and Thomas are both jazz fans.

18 Combine the sentences into one sentence. Use <u>but</u>, <u>both</u>, <u>too</u>, or <u>either</u>.

1. Jen likes rock concerts. Mark doesn't like rock concerts.

   Jen likes rock concerts, but Mark doesn't _____.

2. Chris likes coffee. Lola likes coffee.

   _____.

3. Joon is a new student. Kris isn't a new student.

   _____.

4. Mia doesn't have a large family. Greg doesn't have a large family.

   _____.

5. Jay looks like his father. His brother doesn't look like his father.

   _____.

19 CHALLENGE. **Look at the sports website. Write a paragraph comparing the two famous athletes.**

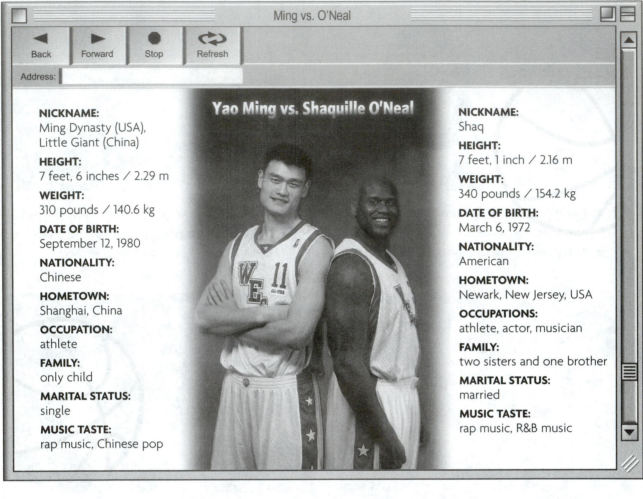

Ming vs. O'Neal

◄ Back   ► Forward   ● Stop   ↻ Refresh

Address:

Yao Ming vs. Shaquille O'Neal

NICKNAME:
Ming Dynasty (USA),
Little Giant (China)

HEIGHT:
7 feet, 6 inches / 2.29 m

WEIGHT:
310 pounds / 140.6 kg

DATE OF BIRTH:
September 12, 1980

NATIONALITY:
Chinese

HOMETOWN:
Shanghai, China

OCCUPATION:
athlete

FAMILY:
only child

MARITAL STATUS:
single

MUSIC TASTE:
rap music, Chinese pop

NICKNAME:
Shaq

HEIGHT:
7 feet, 1 inch / 2.16 m

WEIGHT:
340 pounds / 154.2 kg

DATE OF BIRTH:
March 6, 1972

NATIONALITY:
American

HOMETOWN:
Newark, New Jersey, USA

OCCUPATIONS:
athlete, actor, musician

FAMILY:
two sisters and one brother

MARITAL STATUS:
married

MUSIC TASTE:
rap music, R&B music

GRAMMAR BOOSTER

A Choose the correct response. Write the letter on the line.

1. ____ "Do you and your brothers play soccer together?"
2. ____ "Does your brother work in a restaurant?"
3. ____ "Do your parents like music?"
4. ____ "Does your aunt look like your mother?"
5. ____ "Do you live near here?"
6. ____ "Do I need a tie?"

a. Yes, we do.

b. No, he doesn't.

c. No, I don't.

d. Yes, they do. Very much.

e. No, she doesn't. She looks a little like me.

f. No, you don't.

B Complete the conversations. Write short answers to the questions.

1. A: Does he live in Sydney?

   B: _No, he doesn't_____. He lives in Melbourne.

2. A: Do your friends like Chinese food?

   B: _____. They go to Chinese restaurants all the time.

3. A: Do you have a big family?

   B: _____. I have eight brothers and sisters.

4. A: Does your husband work in an office?

   B: _____. He's a musician.

5. A: Do we need to buy our tickets now?

   B: _____. We can buy our tickets on the train.

C Complete the conversations. Write <u>yes</u> / <u>no</u> questions with the simple present tense.

1. A: He doesn't like concerts.

   B: _Does he like_ _____ movies?

2. A: My sister doesn't eat fish.

   B: _____ meat?

3. A: My grandfather doesn't drink tea.

   B: _____ coffee?

4. A: I don't like rap music.

   B: _____ jazz?

5. A: I have two brothers and one sister.

   B: _____ nieces and nephews?

D Choose the correct response. Circle the letter.

1. "Where do your grandparents live?"
   a. In São Paolo.   b. Yes, they do.   c. I don't think so.

2. "How often do you see your cousins?"
   a. In June.   b. Every month.   c. Yes, I do.

3. "When does he go to school?"
   a. In Mexico City.   b. In the morning.   c. No, he doesn't.

4. "Does your father eat meat?"
   a. No, he doesn't.   b. In the kitchen.   c. At 8 p.m.

5. "What time does your sister go to bed?"
   a. Yes, she does.   b. At midnight.   c. In the evening.

6. "How many people work in that office?"
   a. No, they don't.   b. Twenty or twenty-five.   c. I think so.

7. "Do Mark and Lisa speak Italian?"
   a. Yes, they do.   b. Yes, she does.   c. Italy.

E Look at the responses. Write information questions with the simple present tense.

1. A: _How many brothers and sisters does Anna have_____?
   B: Anna? She has three brothers and one sister.

2. A: _____?
   B: Jon? He works in London.

3. A: _____?
   B: They usually start class at 8:00.

4. A: _____?
   B: Me? I like all kinds of music.

A Riddle for You!

Riddle: Two babies are born at the same time to the same mother, but they're not twins. What are they?

Answer: They're two of a set of triplets!

JUST FOR FUN

1 ▸ Complete the puzzle. Write the letters of each word in the boxes.

Across

1. your brother's son
2. almost the same
3. your mother's sister
4. not married

Down

5. brother-in-_____
6. aunt's or uncle's children
7. not older
8. mother and father
9. two children born at the same time
10. not the same

2 ▸ **BRAINTEASER.** Who's who? Look at the family photos. Write the names under the pictures. Use the hints and the names in the list.

Hints:

Shirley is Ted's grandmother.
Kelly is an only child.
Rick is married to Beth.
Cynthia has two nephews and one niece.
Mark and Barbara have two children.
Harry is Beth's father-in-law.
Cynthia is Barbara's sister.
Alex is Ted's older brother.

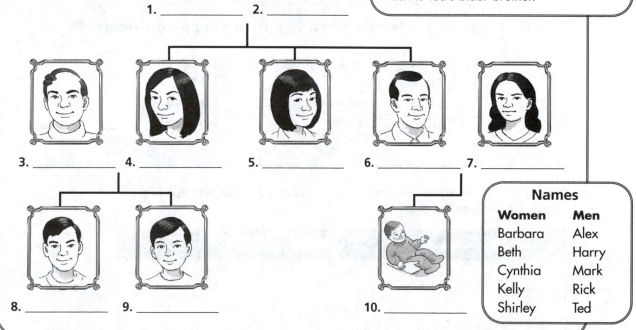

The Clark Family Tree

1. _____ 2. _____

3. _____ 4. _____ 5. _____ 6. _____ 7. _____

8. _____ 9. _____ 10. _____

Names

Women	Men
Barbara	Alex
Beth	Harry
Cynthia	Mark
Kelly	Rick
Shirley	Ted

Coping with Technology

TOPIC PREVIEW

1 Look at the ads from a shopping catalog. Then check ✓ <u>true</u>, <u>false</u>, or <u>no information</u> based on the information given in the catalog.

ALL-STAR SPORTS WATCH

This tough digital watch is truly amazing! Perfect for playing sports, exercising, even swimming! It's waterproof to 1,000 meters. The large, easy to read display shows the day, month, and year. Only US$30! Order now!

Traveler 3000 Watch

Available here only! Do you travel often? Then the Traveler 3000 is the watch for you! Watch features two analog faces, so it's easy to see the time in two different time zones. Displays the day of the week. Your choice of silver, gold, or black face. Order yours today—only US$60!

	true	false	no information
1. The Traveler 3000 watch tells the day of the week.	☐	☐	☐
2. The All-Star Sports watch is a lemon.	☐	☐	☐
3. The Traveler 3000 watch costs US$3,000.	☐	☐	☐
4. Both watches tell the month and year.	☐	☐	☐

2 Take the survey about shopping catalogs.

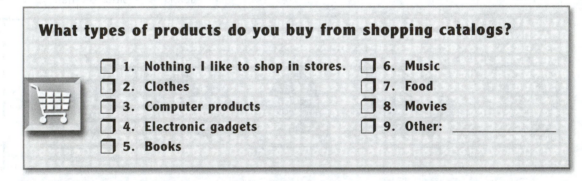

What types of products do you buy from shopping catalogs?

- ☐ 1. Nothing. I like to shop in stores.
- ☐ 2. Clothes
- ☐ 3. Computer products
- ☐ 4. Electronic gadgets
- ☐ 5. Books
- ☐ 6. Music
- ☐ 7. Food
- ☐ 8. Movies
- ☐ 9. Other: _____

3 WHAT ABOUT YOU? Which gadgets or machines do you like? Which don't you like? Complete the chart.

Machines and gadgets I like	Machines and gadgets I don't like

LESSON 1

4 ▸ **Choose the correct response. Circle the letter.**

1. "I'm looking for a new cell phone. Do you have any suggestions?"
   a. No, it's just a lemon.   b. Yes, it does.   c. How about a Global Mobile?

2. "What's wrong with your MP3 player?"
   a. It won't play.   b. It's expensive.   c. It's busy right now.

3. "What are you doing here?"
   a. I'm looking for a printer.   b. I'm not home right now.   c. It's printing.

4. "My laptop isn't working."
   a. It's terrific.   b. Any suggestions?   c. What's wrong with it?

5 ▸ **Complete each conversation with the present continuous.**

What _is George doing_ here?
1. George / do

I think _____ for a new TV.
2. he / look

His TV _____.
3. not work

_____ to your
4. you / go
sister's house this weekend?

Yes, I am. _____ at 2:00.
5. I / leave

Who _____?
6. you / call

My brother-in-law. But his phone is busy.
I think _____ the Internet.
7. he / use

6 **Read the questions. Write answers starting with No. Use the information in parentheses.**

1. Is he leaving at 10:30? (11:00)

   No, he isn't. He's leaving at 11:00.

2. Are they studying for an exam? (look at a catalog)

   _____.

3. Are you shopping for a laptop? (a PDA)

   _____.

4. Is she going to the movie at 8:00? (7:30)

   _____.

7 **Write questions starting with Is or Are.**

1. you / look for / a new computer

   _Are you looking for a new computer_____?

2. he / use / the computer / now

   _____?

3. they / buy / a CD burner

   _____?

4. Karla / work / today

   _____?

8 **Look at the responses. Complete the questions. Use the present continuous.**

1. **A:** What _are you looking for_____?

   B: I'm looking for a dictionary.

2. **A:** Who _____?

   B: Tom is going to the computer show.

3. **A:** What _____?

   B: I'm buying a new CD.

4. **A:** When _____?

   B: My sister is going to Vienna in June.

9 Look at Maria's PDA. Answer the questions about her schedule. Use the present continuous.

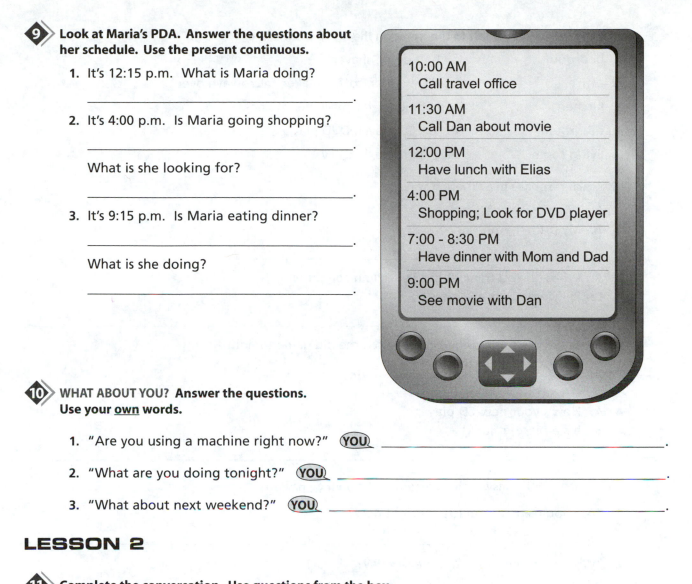

1. It's 12:15 p.m. What is Maria doing?

_____.

2. It's 4:00 p.m. Is Maria going shopping?

_____.

What is she looking for?

_____.

3. It's 9:15 p.m. Is Maria eating dinner?

_____.

What is she doing?

_____.

10:00 AM
Call travel office

11:30 AM
Call Dan about movie

12:00 PM
Have lunch with Elias

4:00 PM
Shopping; Look for DVD player

7:00 - 8:30 PM
Have dinner with Mom and Dad

9:00 PM
See movie with Dan

10 WHAT ABOUT YOU? Answer the questions. Use your <u>own</u> words.

1. "Are you using a machine right now?" (YOU) _____.

2. "What are you doing tonight?" (YOU) _____.

3. "What about next weekend?" (YOU) _____.

LESSON 2

11 Complete the conversation. Use questions from the box.

What's wrong with it?	How's it going?	Any suggestions?	What brand is it?

A: Hi, Ed. _____
      1.

B: OK, thanks. But my coffee maker's driving me crazy!

A: Not again! _____
      2.

B: I don't know. It just isn't working. This thing is a piece of junk!

A: That's too bad. _____
      3.

B: It's a Coffee Pal 300.

A: Sounds like you need a new coffee maker.

B: That's for sure. _____
      4.

A: Well, how about a Brewtech? The model that I have is terrific!

B: Really? Thanks for the suggestion.

12 Match the rooms on the left to the items on the right. Draw a line.

1. bedroom   a. hair dryer, shaver

2. office   b. dishwasher, coffee maker, microwave oven

3. kitchen   c. computer, fax machine, copier

4. bathroom   d. TV, CD player, DVD player

5. living room   e. telephone, bed, TV

13 Write each response in a different way.

1. **A:** What's wrong?
   B: My printer won't print.

   My printer's not working .

2. **A:** What do you think about Pell brand computers?
   B: Pell computers are great!

   _____ !

3. **A:** My TV isn't working. I can't watch the big game tonight.
   B: I'm sorry to hear that.

   _____ .

4. **A:** How's your new CD player?
   B: It's a piece of junk!

   _____ !

14 WHAT ABOUT YOU? Answer the questions. Use your **own** words.

1. "Are you using any machines right now?"

   YOU _____ .

2. "What machines do you use every day?"

   YOU _____ .

3. "What machines do you never use? Why not?"

   YOU _____ .

LESSONS 3 AND 4

15 Look at the chart. Read the statements. Check ✔ **true**, **false**, or **no information**.

Country	Cell phones*	Radios*	Personal computers*		true	false	no information
Brazil	25	403	48	1. Cell phones are not popular in Brazil.	☐	☐	☐
France	185	925	300	2. Personal computers are very popular in Portugal.	☐	☐	☐
Iceland	888	931	394				
Japan	503	949	315				
Portugal	305	299	104	3. 931 people have radios in Iceland.	☐	☐	☐
U.K.	728	1,414	338				
U.S.A.	247	2,049	574	4. Radios are expensive in the U.K.	☐	☐	☐
*per 1,000 people							

SOURCE: CIA World Factbook, 2002

16 ► **Look at the picture. Then complete the paragraph. Use the present continuous.**

It's a busy Monday morning at the office of Techco Inc. The company president, Ms. Cline,

<u>is answering</u> her e-mail. She _____ tomorrow morning. She _____ to Brazil for a
 1. answer   2. leave   3. go

sales meeting. Her assistant, Frank, _____ on the phone right now. He _____ Ms.
                                      4. talk   5. buy

Cline's airplane tickets. Jim, a sales manager, _____ the photocopier and the fax machine.
                                                 6. use

He _____ copies of a report for the meeting and _____ a fax to Ms. Cline's hotel.
   7. make   8. send

Jeff and Aliza also work for Techco. They _____ the break room and _____ coffee.
                                          9. clean   10. make

17 ► **Look at the picture. Find all of the problems in the office. Write a short paragraph about the problems.**

The employees at the Techco office are having problems . . .

_____

_____

_____

_____

Presenting the Sony, er . . . Stowaway?

Mr. Akio Morita and Mr. Masaru Ibuka started the Sony Corporation in Tokyo in 1946. At first, Sony was a small electrical repair company. In 1953, they started to sell the first transistor radios. In 1979, Sony introduced one of their most famous products, the "Walkman" portable cassette player.

Sony engineers invented the Walkman after they noticed young Japanese people listening to music all day, even carrying large stereos to the park. They believed that people wanted a music player that was small enough to wear in a shirt pocket. Sony also wanted the cassette player to be easy to use, so that people could listen to music while doing other things like exercising, riding the train, or doing housework.

**Sony Walkman ™
Cassette Player**

Sony chose the name "Walkman" for their new product. At first, the Walkman didn't sell well. Electronic stores didn't think people would buy it. Some thought that the Walkman would make people unfriendly and stop talking to other people. However, as more people heard about the Walkman, it became a big hit. Japanese music fans loved it. When Sony was ready to sell the Walkman in other countries, they worried that people would think that the name was bad English. They made plans to call it the "Soundabout" in the United States and the "Stowaway" in the United Kingdom. But Mr. Morita wanted his gadget to have the same name in every country, and today "Walkman" is its name all over the world. You can even find "walkman" in the dictionary! Since 1979, there have been 300 different Walkman models and over 150 million have been sold around the world. The Sony Walkman is now the best selling consumer electronics product ever made.

SOURCE: www.sony.net

Now read the article again. According to the information in the article, which adjectives describe the Sony Walkman?

☐ convenient
☐ guaranteed
☐ expensive
☐ fast
☐ portable
☐ popular

19 WRITING. Do you think that the Walkman is a good product? Why or why not? Write a short paragraph.

GRAMMAR
BOOSTER

A Change each statement from the simple present tense to the present continuous. Use contractions.

1. I eat breakfast every morning.

   I'm eating breakfast _____ now.

2. My mother buys a newspaper every day.

   _____ now.

3. They walk to school every day.

   _____ now.

4. It rains all the time in the summer.

   _____ now.

5. The bus stops in front of my house at 2 p.m.

   _____ now.

6. He runs in the park every afternoon.

   _____ now.

7. We close the store at 5 p.m.

   _____ now.

8. He writes the report on Fridays.

   _____ now.

B Write negative statements. Use the words in parentheses.

1. He's going to school now. _He's not working_ _____. (work)

2. Sonia and Lee are drinking water. _____. (tea)

3. Ted is writing a letter. _____. (do homework)

4. You're talking a lot. _____. (listen)

5. I'm reading a magazine. _____. (a book)

6. We're eating at my house. _____. (your house)

7. The fax machine is making a noise. _____. (print)

C Choose the correct response. Write the letter on the line.

1. ____ "Are you going to work now?"   a. A new coffee maker.

2. ____ "Is he studying for an English test?" b. No, he's not.

3. ____ "Where are you sitting?"   c. Next to Susana.

4. ____ "What is Tina buying?"   d. Yes, I am.

5. ____ "Are they listening to jazz?"   e. He's leaving in an hour.

6. ____ "When is he leaving work?"   f. Yuko and Miyumi.

7. ____ "Who's watching TV?"   g. No, they aren't. It's rap.

◆ **D** **Write questions. Use the present continuous.**

1. go / to the store / who

   Who is going to the store ?

2. they / play soccer / where

   _____?

3. Sam / eat / what

   _____?

4. when / Lidia / come home

   _____?

5. my computer / why / use / you

   _____?

JUST FOR **FUN**

◆ **1** **Look at the pictures. Write the words. Then look at the gray boxes** ☐.

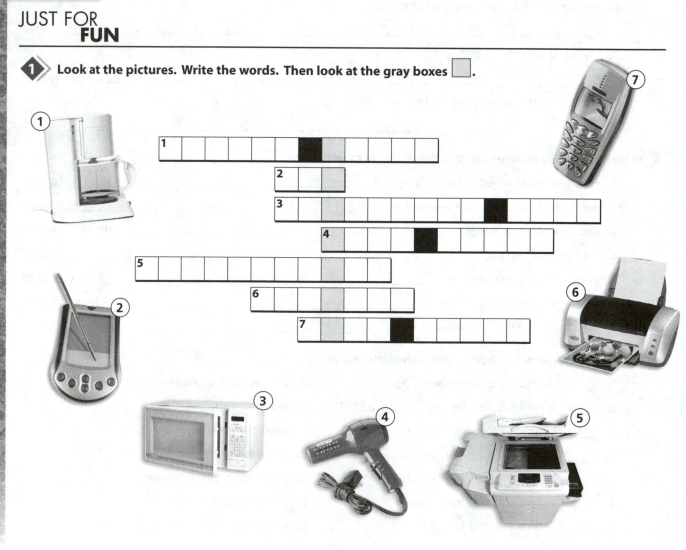

What's the new word? _____

2 Read about the machines. Then write the name of the machine on the line.

1. You use this machine to cook food and heat beverages fast. This first model is from 1947. It weighs over 750 pounds (340 kg). Today's models weigh just 25 pounds (11.3 kg)!

   What is it?

   a microwave oven

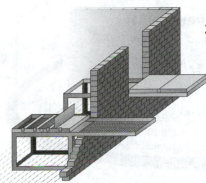

2. You can find this machine in almost every office. This model is from 1886. To use it, you open a window and put the machine outside. On a cloudy day, it takes one hour to make one copy! Today, these machines make hundreds of copies in seconds. And you don't have to open a window!

   What is it?

   _____

3. People use this machine on wet hair. This early model is from 1920. It is made of metal and is very heavy. It's not easy to use. Today's plastic models are light, easy to use, and portable.

   What is it?

   _____

4. This appliance is used to keep food cold. This 1916 model is called an "ice box," because you have to put big pieces of ice inside. Today's model has a different name, and you don't have to buy any ice!

   What is it?

   _____

You mean it's not a coffee cup holder?

Eating in, Eating out

TOPIC PREVIEW

1 Look at the menus. Then read the conversations. Where are the customers eating? Write the name of the restaurant on the line.

Louis' Restaurant

Appetizers Shrimp salad
Tomato soup

Entrées
All entrées come with a choice of soup or salad.
Grilled steak
Fried clams

Desserts Fruit salad
Chocolate cream pie

Beverages Coffee   Tea (iced or hot)
Fruit juice   Soft drinks

CLEO'S CAFÉ

APPETIZERS
Green salad   Chicken soup

ENTRÉES
Fried chicken   Grilled fish

DESSERTS
Ice cream
(choice of Chocolate or Vanilla)
Apple pie

BEVERAGES
Coffee   Tea   Soft drinks
Bottled water

Are you ready to order?

Yes, thanks. I'll have the fried chicken.

Would you like to start with an appetizer?

Yes, I'd like a green salad.

1. _Cleo's Café_

2. _____

What comes with the entrées?

You have a choice of soup or salad.

Anything to drink?

Fruit juice, please.

3. _____

4. _____

WHAT ABOUT YOU? Look at the menus in Exercise 1 again. Where will you eat? What food will you order?

> I'll eat at _____. I'll start with the _____.
> Then I'll have the _____. I'll have _____ to drink,
> and _____ for dessert.

LESSON 1

3 Complete the word webs. Write food categories and foods on the lines.

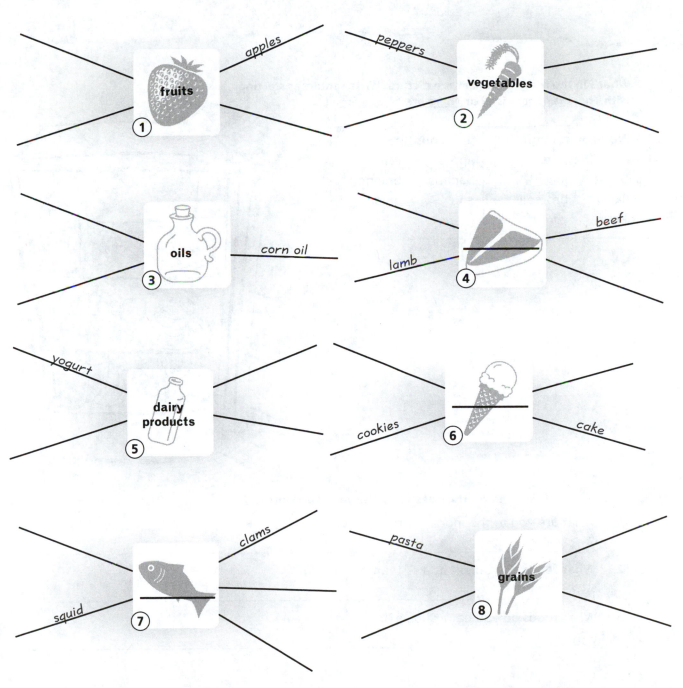

4 Read the note. What foods does Nelson need? Write Nelson's shopping list.

Hi Nelson,

Can you stop at the supermarket this evening? We don't have anything to eat! There's no milk and we're out of fruit. Can you get a chicken and some vegetables (carrots, potatoes, peppers)? We'll have chicken soup for dinner. I'm in the mood to cook!

Thanks,

Kathy

<u>Shopping List</u>

5 What's in the fridge? Look at the picture. Write sentences starting with <u>There is</u> / <u>There isn't</u> or <u>There are</u> / <u>There aren't</u>.

Non-count nouns		Count nouns	
fish	lettuce	apple	carrot
sausage	juice	banana	orange
milk	broccoli	egg	onion
cheese	yogurt	grape	

6 WHAT ABOUT YOU? Answer the questions. Use your <u>own</u> words.

1. "What are you in the mood for right now?"

   YOU _____.

2. "What foods do you eat at a restaurant?"

   YOU _____.

3. "What foods do you eat at home?"

   YOU _____.

LESSON 2

7 ▸ **Match the statement on the left with the explanation on the right. Draw a line.**

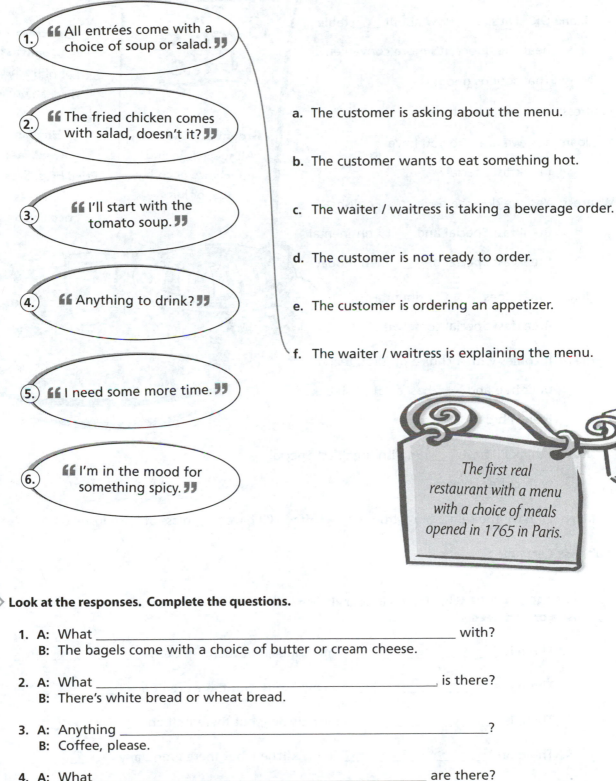

1. "All entrées come with a choice of soup or salad."

2. "The fried chicken comes with salad, doesn't it?"

3. "I'll start with the tomato soup."

4. "Anything to drink?"

5. "I need some more time."

6. "I'm in the mood for something spicy."

a. The customer is asking about the menu.

b. The customer wants to eat something hot.

c. The waiter / waitress is taking a beverage order.

d. The customer is not ready to order.

e. The customer is ordering an appetizer.

f. The waiter / waitress is explaining the menu.

The first real restaurant with a menu with a choice of meals opened in 1765 in Paris.

8 ▸ **Look at the responses. Complete the questions.**

1. **A:** What _____ with?
   B: The bagels come with a choice of butter or cream cheese.

2. **A:** What _____, is there?
   B: There's white bread or wheat bread.

3. **A:** Anything _____?
   B: Coffee, please.

4. **A:** What _____ are there?
   B: Today we have ice cream, fruit salad, and apple pie.

9 Complete the conversations with **a**, **an**, or **the**.

Mary: Let's get ____ table.
   1.

Joan: OK. Let's see. How about ____ table
   2.
near the door? It's more convenient.

Mary: That sounds good.

Waitress: Are you ready to order?

Joan: Yes, we are. Do you have ____
   3.
breakfast special?

Waitress: Yes, we do. We have ____ English
   4.
Breakfast Special and ____ Continental
   5.
Breakfast Special on ____ menu today.
   6.

Joan: What does ____ Continental
   7.
Breakfast Special come with?

Waitress: It comes with a choice of juice, tea,
or coffee and ____ basket of fresh-baked
   8.
French bread.

Joan: I think I'll have ____ English Breakfast Special
   9.
with coffee, please.

Mary: I'll have the same, but without ____ coffee. I'll have ____ glass of juice instead.
   10.   11.

Waitress: Certainly.

The Sunrise Café

Breakfast Specials:
All specials include
your choice of coffee,
tea, or juice.

Continental Breakfast
Basket of fresh-baked
French bread

English Breakfast
Fried Eggs, Sausage,
Tomatoes,
Fried Potatoes

10 WHAT ABOUT YOU? **What food is in your kitchen? Complete the sentences.**
Use **a** or **an** if needed.

1. There is _____ in my fridge, but there isn't any _____.

2. There are _____ in my fridge, but there aren't any _____.

3. There is _____ in my kitchen, but there isn't any _____.

4. There are _____ in my kitchen, but there aren't any _____.

LESSONS 3 AND 4

11 Look at the menu. Then answer the questions with short answers.

1. Does the pasta come with a salad?

   _Yes, it does_____.

2. What kind of soup is there?

   _____.

3. Is there any seafood on the menu?

   _____.

4. Are there any healthy foods on the menu?

   _____.

5. Is the fish entrée spicy?

   _____.

6. Does this restaurant accept credit cards?

   _____.

7. What kind of salad is there?

   _____.

JACK'S RESTAURANT

SOUPS
Clam Chowder   Chicken Vegetable

SALADS
Pasta Salad   Mixed Green Salad

ENTRÉES
ALL ENTRÉES INCLUDE A CHOICE OF SOUP OR SALAD.
Teriyaki Steak with mashed potatoes
Vegetable Beef Stew with carrots, potatoes, and peas
Pasta with tomato sauce
Grilled Fish with garlic and red pepper sauce

LITE ENTRÉES
Low-Fat Baked Chicken with cottage cheese and fresh fruit
Vegetable Sandwich—sweet bell peppers, cucumbers, carrots, and mixed salad greens on pita bread

BEVERAGES
Bottled Water   Soft Drinks   Tea   Coffee

= This is a hot dish!

SORRY, WE DO NOT ACCEPT CREDIT CARDS.

12 Create a menu for the Healthy Choice Café. Write healthful foods that you like to eat under each menu category.

Healthy Choice Café
"EAT OUT WITH US AND EAT SMART!"

Appetizers
_Raw Veggie Platter_____

_____

_____

_____

Soups

_____

_____

_____

Entrées

_____

_____

_____

_____

Desserts

_____

_____

_____

Beverages

_____

_____

_____

A ▸ Complete the chart with nouns from the box.

~~rain~~	~~apple~~	cookie
water	fun	fish
fruit	cheese	bread
help	egg	onion

COUNT	NON-COUNT
apple	*rain*

B ▸ **WHAT ABOUT YOU?** Write <u>How much</u> or <u>How many</u> to complete the questions. Then answer each question using a countable quantity. Use your <u>own</u> words.

1. "_____ eggs do you buy each week?"

   (YOU) _____.

2. "_____ rain do you get in a year?"

   (YOU) _____.

3. "_____ fish is in your refrigerator?"

   (YOU) _____.

4. "_____ apples do you eat in a month?"

   (YOU) _____.

5. "_____ milk do you drink every week?"

   (YOU) _____.

Complete the e-mail. Write <u>a</u> or <u>an</u> in front of count nouns or <u>X</u> in front of non-count nouns.

Brad,

I need _X_ help with dinner today. Can you go to the
    1.

store and buy _____ liter of milk and _____ loaf of bread?
      2.   **3.**

We also need _____ onion or two, and _____ kilo of apples.
        4.   **5.**

Do you think we have _____ cheese? If not, please get
           6.

_____ package of that, too. I'll see you at home after 5:00.
7.

Tracy

Complete the conversations with <u>some</u> or <u>any</u>. For some items, more than one answer may be possible.

1. **A:** Do you need _____ bread?

   B: No, thanks. I have _____.

2. **A:** Do they want _____ soup?

   B: No, they don't want _____ right now.

3. **A:** I don't have _____ water and I'm so thirsty.

   B: Do you want _____ tea?

4. **A:** Does she need _____ help?

   B: She doesn't need _____ help. She needs _____ practice.

1 Read the sentences. Write the words. Then look at the gray boxes ▢.

1. You can have soup or a salad. It's your _____.

2. Eat foods from the _____ group in moderation.

3. It's not a good idea to eat a lot of _____ between meals.

4. Some people eat five or six small _____ a day.

5. Meat and cheese are _____ foods.

6. Fried foods and sweets can be _____ in fat and sugar.

1. | c | | | | | e |

2. | s | w | | | s |

3. | s | n | | | s |

4. | m | | | s |

5. | f | | | y |

6. | h | i | |

What's the new word? _____

2 What is it? Write the word on the line.

1. The waiter gives it to you at a restaurant. You read it to order food.
   It's a _____.

2. You eat them before your entrée. They are _____.

3. It's a healthy food group. Oranges and apples are in it. It's _____.

4. The waiter gives it to you after you eat. You can pay it with a credit card.
   It's the _____.

5. It's the amount of a food that you eat in one meal. It's a _____.

6. It's a very cold dessert. It's _____.

IMAGES: <u>budgetstockphoto.com</u>

UNIT 6

Staying in Shape

TOPIC PREVIEW

1 ▶ **Look at the pictures. Name each activity. Write the letter on the line.**

1. ___ swimming
2. ___ walking
3. ___ doing aerobics
4. ___ dancing
5. ___ playing soccer
6. ___ playing the guitar
7. ___ running
8. ___ lifting weights
9. ___ sleeping

2 ▶ **WHAT ABOUT YOU?** How often do you do these activities? Complete the chart.

Activity	Frequency
ride a bike	
eat in a restaurant	
shop for clothes	
shop for food	
watch TV	
clean your house	
exercise	

LESSON 1

3 ▶ **Choose the correct response. Circle the letter.**

1. "Can you go walking at 4:30?"
   a. Yes, I am.
   b. No, I can't.
   c. Yes, I do.

2. "Why don't we go dancing tonight at 8:00?"
   a. OK. When's good for you?
   b. Sorry, I can't.
   c. Too bad.

3. "When do you have to go to work?"
   a. No, I'm not busy.
   b. How about tomorrow at 6:00?
   c. At 10:30.

4. "When's good for you?"
   a. How about Monday morning?
   b. Sounds good!
   c. Sorry, I can't.

4 ▶ **Complete the sentences. Use <u>have to</u> or <u>has to</u>.**

1. I _____ go to class this morning. Do you have my textbook?

2. She can sleep late tomorrow morning. She doesn't _____ work until 10:30.

3. My brother isn't healthy. He _____ exercise more.

4. They don't _____ pick us up at the train station. We can take a taxi.

5. Pete _____ buy a new digital camera. His old one isn't working.

6. Do you _____ work next Saturday?

7. We _____ finish our report before the next sales meeting.

5 ▷ **Write sentences. Use words from each box.**

I		has to		work late on Friday.
My parents		don't have to		play tennis this weekend.
My teacher	**+**	can	**+**	go to school.
My friend		can't		study English.
My boss		have to		go shopping this weekend.
My brother		doesn't have to		cook dinner tonight.
				sleep late tomorrow morning.

1. _My brother doesn't have to study English_____.

2. _____.

3. _____.

4. _____.

5. _____.

6 ▷ **Look at Paula's daily planner. Answer the questions about her schedule.**

1. Can Paula go running Saturday morning at 9:00?

   _No, she can't. She has to____

   _study English_____.

2. What does Paula have to do on Sunday afternoon?

   _____

   _____.

3. Does Paula have to work on Friday?

   _____

   _____.

4. Why can't Paula do aerobics Sunday night at 7:30?

   _____

   _____.

5. Can Paula sleep late on Sunday morning?

   _____

   _____.

	FRIDAY	SATURDAY	SUNDAY
9:00			

Daily Planner

	FRIDAY	SATURDAY	SUNDAY
9:00	Arrive at the office	English class	
11:00			
1:00	Sales meeting	Lunch with Dad	Clean the house
3:00			
5:00	Leave the office	Shop for a new cell phone	Cook dinner
7:00	Do aerobics		See a movie with Sara

7 ▸ **Look at the responses. Write questions with <u>can</u> or <u>have to</u>.**

1. **A:** (Gail / speak Polish) *Can Gail speak Polish* _____?

   B: No. She speaks English and French.

2. **A:** (you / play basketball tonight) _____?

   B: Sure. I'm not busy.

3. **A:** (you / meet your brother at the airport) _____?

   B: No, I don't. He's taking a bus.

4. **A:** (I / call you tomorrow) _____?

   B: OK. That would be great.

5. **A:** (Frank / buy a new printer) _____?

   B: No. He fixed his old one.

6. **A:** (they / take the exam on Friday) _____?

   B: Yes, they do. They're studying tonight.

LESSON 2

8 ▸ **Complete the sentences with places from the box.**

gym   athletic field   pool   court   track   course

1. The school _____ is used for a lot of different sports. Students play

   football and soccer in the fall and baseball in the spring.

2. You can take an aerobics class or use exercise machines at a _____.

3. The hotel has a tennis _____ and an 18-hole golf _____.

4. On Fridays, there are water aerobics classes in the swimming _____.

5. You can go running or walking on a _____.

9 ▸ **Choose the correct response. Write the letter on the line.**

1. ____ "How often do you do aerobics?"

2. ____ "How often do you go swimming?"

3. ____ "When do you go dancing?"

4. ____ "What are you doing this weekend?"

5. ____ "How come you're not going running

   tonight?"

6. ____ "Are you studying right now?"

a. Because I'm too busy.

b. I go to the gym once a week.

c. No, I'm not. I'm watching TV.

d. I'm going shopping on Saturday and
   sleeping late on Sunday.

e. I hardly ever go to the pool.

f. On Friday nights.

10 Look at Dave's activity schedule for September. Then complete the sentences. Circle the letter.

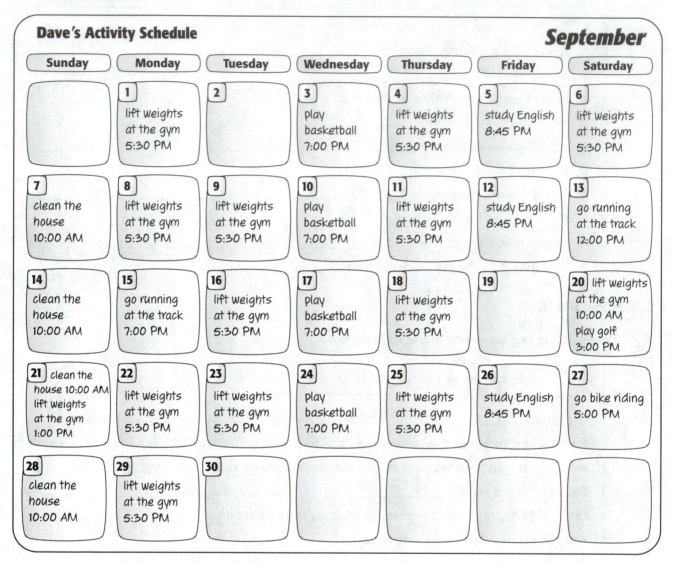

Dave's Activity Schedule   *September*

Sunday	Monday	Tuesday	Wednesday	Thursday	Friday	Saturday
	1 lift weights at the gym 5:30 PM	**2**	**3** play basketball 7:00 PM	**4** lift weights at the gym 5:30 PM	**5** study English 8:45 PM	**6** lift weights at the gym 5:30 PM
7 clean the house 10:00 AM	**8** lift weights at the gym 5:30 PM	**9** lift weights at the gym 5:30 PM	**10** play basketball 7:00 PM	**11** lift weights at the gym 5:30 PM	**12** study English 8:45 PM	**13** go running at the track 12:00 PM
14 clean the house 10:00 AM	**15** go running at the track 7:00 PM	**16** lift weights at the gym 5:30 PM	**17** play basketball 7:00 PM	**18** lift weights at the gym 5:30 PM	**19**	**20** lift weights at the gym 10:00 AM play golf 3:00 PM
21 clean the house 10:00 AM lift weights at the gym 1:00 PM	**22** lift weights at the gym 5:30 PM	**23** lift weights at the gym 5:30 PM	**24** play basketball 7:00 PM	**25** lift weights at the gym 5:30 PM	**26** study English 8:45 PM	**27** go bike riding 5:00 PM
28 clean the house 10:00 AM	**29** lift weights at the gym 5:30 PM	**30**				

1. Dave _____ goes bike riding.
   a. hardly ever   **b.** never   **c.** always

2. Dave _____ cleans the house on Sundays.
   a. always   **b.** sometimes   **c.** never

3. Dave lifts weights _____.
   a. once a week   **b.** at least three times a week   **c.** once in a while

4. Dave plays basketball _____.
   a. on Tuesdays   **b.** on Wednesdays   **c.** on weekends

5. Dave usually lifts weights _____.
   a. in the evening   **b.** in the morning   **c.** in the afternoon

6. Dave goes running _____.
   a. once a month   **b.** every weekend   **c.** once in a while

11 WHAT ABOUT YOU? Write sentences about your own activities.

Examples: *I hardly ever eat in a restaurant* .
I ride a bike once in a while .

1. _____.
2. _____.
3. _____.
4. _____.
5. _____.

12 Look at the responses. Complete the questions. Use the simple present tense.

1. How often *does Jim play tennis* _____?
   Jim plays tennis every day.

2. How often _____?
   I go walking once in a while.

3. When _____?
   I usually cook dinner at 7:30.

4. When _____?
   They go dancing on Friday nights.

5. Where _____?
   We do aerobics at the gym.

6. Where _____?
   Kyle plays soccer at the athletic field.

13 Write sentences. Use the simple present tense or the present continuous.

1. Charlie / usually / play golf / on weekends
   Charlie usually plays golf on weekends .

2. Stan / talk on the phone / right now

   _____.

3. My daughter / never / study English

   _____.

4. We / go dancing / tonight

   _____.

5. I / sleep late / tomorrow morning

   _____.

6. He / take a shower / now

   _____.

7. They / drive to work / at least once a week

   _____.

8. She / work late / next Tuesday

   _____.

9. I / always / go swimming / on Mondays and Wednesdays

   _____.

14 ▶ **Read the letters to a health magazine advice column.**

Dear In-Shape,

I have two health questions for you. I'm an athlete. I play baseball for my university team and I go running every day. I exercise all the time. I think I'm in terrific shape, but I'm worried that I exercise too much. That's my first question— how much exercise is too much?

My second question is about my diet. I try to eat healthy. I hardly ever eat pizza, fast food, or other snacks. I never drink soft drinks. But I have one really bad habit: I'm crazy about sweets!

I eat too much chocolate, candy, cake, and ice cream. How can I cut down on sweets?

—Ron Miller

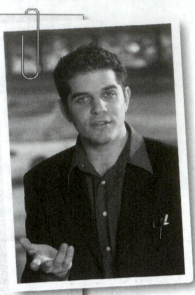

Dear In-Shape,

I need some exercise advice! I don't feel very healthy. I get tired just walking from my house to my car! My doctor said that I have to exercise more. I'm sure that she's right. I should get out of the house more often. My husband goes running every day, but I never go running with him. I'm a couch potato. My big activity is watching movies—I watch a movie just about every night. Unfortunately, you don't burn many calories watching TV!

By the way, the problem is not my diet. I generally try to eat foods that are good for me, like fish, vegetables, and fruit. I avoid snacks and I almost never eat sweets!

—Nina Hunter

Now read the letters again. Complete the chart about Ron and Nina's diet and exercise habits. Check ✔ the boxes.

	Ron Miller	Nina Hunter
is in shape	☐	☐
is out of shape	☐	☐
eats junk food	☐	☐
avoids sweets	☐	☐
has a sweet tooth	☐	☐

15 **Read the sentences about Ron and Nina. Check ✔ true, false, or no information.**

	true	false	no information
1. Ron doesn't have time to exercise.	☐	☐	☐
2. Ron avoids junk food.	☐	☐	☐
3. Ron usually drinks a lot of water.	☐	☐	☐
4. Nina never eats fish.	☐	☐	☐
5. Nina doesn't exercise regularly.	☐	☐	☐
6. Nina doesn't want to eat healthy foods.	☐	☐	☐

16 **WHAT ABOUT YOU? Are you in shape? Do you have a healthy diet? Explain your answers.**

Example: *I don't have a healthy diet. I almost never eat vegetables . . .*

GRAMMAR BOOSTER

A Look at the responses. Write information questions with <u>can</u>.

1. **A:** _Where can I go running_ ?

   B: Well, you can run in the park.

2. **A:** _____?

   B: I think she can come after class, but I'm not sure.

3. **A:** _____?

   B: Three. I speak Spanish, English, and Japanese.

4. **A:** _____?

   B: I can meet you at 9:30.

5. **A:** _____?

   B: Not very often. Golf is so expensive around here.

B Look at the responses. Write information questions with <u>have to</u>.

1. **A:** _How often do you have to_ _____ see your doctor?

   B: Not very often. Just once a year.

2. **A:** _____ meet the client tomorrow?

   B: I have to meet him at the airport.

3. **A:** _____ pick up the car?

   B: You have to pick it up before 5:00. They close early today.

4. **A:** _____ work late tonight?

   B: Because she has a big meeting tomorrow.

5. **A:** _____ get at the supermarket?

   B: We have to get some chicken and onions for dinner tonight.

C Complete the sentences. Circle the letter.

1. I _____ about lunch. What do you want?
   a. think   **b.** am thinking   **c.** thinks

2. He _____ her very much now.
   a. love   **b.** is loving   **c.** loves

3. Michelle can't come to the phone. She _____.
   a. sleep   **b.** sleeping   **c.** is sleeping

4. They _____ the chef at that restaurant.
   a. are knowing   **b.** know   **c.** am knowing

5. We _____ some soup for dinner. Do you want some?
   a. am having   **b.** has   **c.** are having

Write sentences in the simple present tense.

1. she / a lot / swimming / not / go

   She doesn't go swimming a lot   .

2. walk / Joel / to school / every day

   _____ .

3. every week / not / my sisters / me / call

   _____ .

4. every day / meet / not / their class

   _____ .

5. they / play tennis / three times a week

   _____ .

JUST FOR FUN

1 ▶ **Complete the crossword puzzle.**

Across

1. don't do something because it's bad for you

2. where you play tennis

3. ball game popular around the world

4. a place for indoor exercise

5. 0% of the time

Down

1. 100% of the time

6. where "potatoes" sit

7. exercise on a bike

8. the foods you eat

9. where you play golf

2 Which game or sport uses these? Write the activity or sport on the line.

1. _____

2. _____

3. _____

4. _____

5. _____

6. _____

What is the number one sport in the world? Many people say soccer is the world's most popular sport. In 2002, 1.5 billion people watched the World Cup soccer games on TV. That's one out of every four people in the world!

It's a good clothes rack, and you can use it for exercising, too!

A JOKE FOR YOU!

UNIT 7

Finding Something to Wear

TOPIC PREVIEW

1 Look at the shopping website. Which department would you click to buy these clothing items? Match the department with the item. Write the letter on the line.

Shop at Home Online Department Store

Large selection of fine brand-name clothes **FOR THE WHOLE FAMILY!**

shop at home
ONLINE DEPARTMENT STORE

". . . Just click your mouse. Stay in your house."®

SIGN IN | REGISTER | MY ACCOUNT | CUSTOMER SERVICE | CHECKOUT | VIEW CART

DEPARTMENTS | SPECIALS | OUTERWEAR | HOSIERY | SLEEPWEAR | BAGS and ACCESSORIES | ATHLETIC WEAR

1. _F_ ☞ Bags and Accessories

2. ____ ☞ Men's Underwear

3. ____ ☞ Men's Sleepwear

4. ____ ☞ Hosiery

5. ____ ☞ Women's Sleepwear

6. ____ ☞ Athletic Wear

7. ____ ☞ Outerwear

SEARCH [____] GO

THIS WEEK'S SPECIALS
Click on items for special prices and other details.

Ⓐ Jackets   Ⓑ Socks and Tights   Ⓔ Nightgowns

Ⓒ Men's Boxers   Ⓓ Men's Pajamas

Ⓕ Leather Bags and Belts   Ⓖ Running Shoes, Shorts, and Sweatpants

HOME | OTHER PRODUCTS & SERVICES | GIFT CARDS | CATALOGS | ABOUT US | CONTACT US

2 What's important to these customers when they shop for footwear? Write <u>price</u>, <u>selection</u>, or <u>service</u> on the line.

I always shop at Dalton's Department Store because the clerks are really helpful. They always help me find the right size and even offer to gift wrap!

I'm a student so I don't have a lot of money. I shop at Shoe Outlet because they always have a big sale. The shoes I'm wearing now were 50% off!

Jake's Footwear is the best! They have more than 200 different kinds of footwear— boots, sandals, running shoes . . . I like to have a lot of choices when I shop.

1. _____   2. _____   3. _____

LESSON 1

3 Choose the correct response. Circle the letter.

1. "Do you have this in a medium?"
   a. No, thanks.
   b. Yes, here you go.
   c. Yes, please.

2. "See if these are larger."
   a. Yes, they're OK.
   b. They're $39.
   c. That's too bad.

3. "How much are the pajamas?"
   a. The Sleepy brand ones?
   b. They're too small.
   c. This one's a medium.

4. "Can I try it on?"
   a. Of course!
   b. No, I'm sorry. We don't.
   c. We have a smaller size in black.

4 Complete the chart with words from the box. Write the comparative form of each adjective in the correct column.

loose	spicy	hot	sweet	comfortable
tall	bad	important	thin	young
friendly	healthy	nice	fat	convenient

1. (+) -r	2. (+) -er	3. (-) -y (+) -ier	4. double the final consonant (+) -er	5. more	6. irregular forms
larger	smaller	heavier	bigger	more expensive	better
					X
X					X

5 Compare the items in the pictures. Write sentences with comparative adjectives. Use words from the box or your <u>own</u> words.

spicy	salty	expensive	portable	young
old	cheap	fast	healthy	large
big	small	comfortable	good	convenient

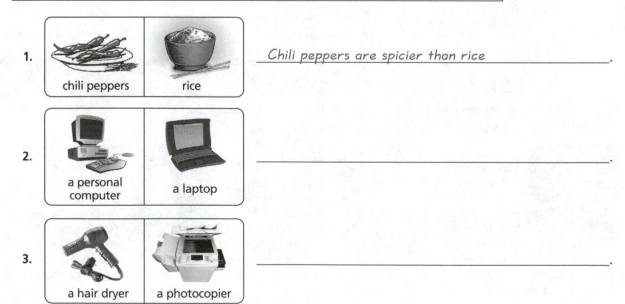

1. chili peppers / rice — Chili peppers are spicier than rice.

2. a personal computer / a laptop — _____.

3. a hair dryer / a photocopier — _____.

4. _____.

running shoes | pumps

5. _____.

your grandparents | your children

6. _____.

a salad | french fries

7. _____.

a microwave oven | a conventional oven

6 Look at the store ad. Then complete the sentences. Use the information in the ad or your <u>own</u> words.

Big City Footwear

BIG BOOT SALE!

Comfort brand casual boots
Light and very comfortable, perfect for walking!
Available in men's US sizes 7 – 14.
Light Brown, Dark Blue, Black

US$25.00

A great low price!

Arctic brand winter boots
Your feet will thank you in cold weather!
Waterproof and heavy weight for safety
on ice and snow.
Available in men's US sizes 7, 12, 13, 14.
Dark Brown, Black

US$55.00

Warm, warm, warm!

Downtown brand dress boots
Knee-high, 3 inch (7.6 cm) heel.
Be fashionable going out or
going to work!
Available in women's US sizes 5 – 10.
Black, Dark Red, Grey, Dark Green

US$90.00

1. The Comfort brand boots are _____ than the Downtown boots.

2. The Big City Footwear store has the Arctic brand boots in brown and _____.

3. The Downtown brand boots are _____ than the Arctic brand boots.

4. The Arctic brand boots are _____ than the Comfort brand boots.

5. The Big City Footwear store has the Downtown brand boots in sizes _____.

7 **WHAT ABOUT YOU?** **Complete the sentences. Use your <u>own</u> ideas and the cues in parentheses.**

1. A _____ is more expensive than a _____. (two electronic products)

2. _____ is too spicy for me. (food)

3. The movie _____ is better than _____. (two movies)

4. _____ is more beautiful than _____. (two actresses)

5. _____ is warmer than _____ in my city. (two months)

6. A size _____ shoe is too large for me. (a shoe size)

LESSON 2

8 **Complete the conversations. Use sentences from the box.**

| Certainly.   Charge, please.   The V-neck or the crew neck?   That's too bad. |

Could you gift wrap these shirts?

CASH

1. _____
_____

Did you know that . . .

■ the first known pictures of footwear are boots in a 15,000-year-old painting in a cave in Spain?

■ in the year 200, Marcus Aurelius, Emperor of Rome, said that only he could wear red sandals?

■ before the 1860s, pairs of boots didn't have a right and a left? Both boots were the same.

How would you like to pay?

2. _____
_____

I'll take the sweater.

3. _____
_____

I'm sorry. We don't have these pumps in black.

4. _____
_____

9 ▷ Label the clothing items in the picture. Use words from the box.

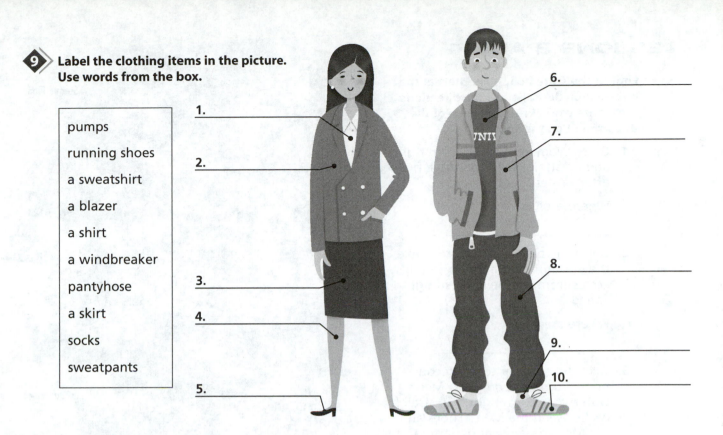

| pumps |
| running shoes |
| a sweatshirt |
| a blazer |
| a shirt |
| a windbreaker |
| pantyhose |
| a skirt |
| socks |
| sweatpants |

1. _____
2. _____
3. _____
4. _____
5. _____
6. _____
7. _____
8. _____
9. _____
10. _____

10 ▷ WHAT ABOUT YOU? What's your style? Complete the chart with the clothing and shoes you usually wear.

At home	At work	At school

11 ▷ Complete the conversations. Use object pronouns from the box. Pronouns can be used more than once.

| me | you | him | her | it | us | you | them |

1. **A:** Are your sisters going to the party?
   B: I hope so. I invited _____.

2. **A:** This sweatshirt is really old.
   B: That's OK. I wear _____ to exercise.

3. **A:** Did you meet Ms. Jacobs?
   B: Yes, I met _____ this morning.

4. **A:** When can I call you?
   B: Let's see. Call _____ tomorrow. I'll be home all day.

5. **A:** I didn't see you and Emma at the concert.
   B: You didn't see _____? We were right near the stage!

6. **A:** I'll take the sandals.
   B: Great! Would you like me to gift wrap _____ for _____?

7. **A:** These pants are too small.
   B: Give _____ to your brother.
   A: I can't give _____ to _____. He wears a size 32!

LESSONS 3 AND 4

12 Look at the store floor plan. Start at the Information desk. Follow the directions. Where are you? Write the name of the department on the line.

1. Go to Women's Casual. Turn right and go straight. It's on the left side, after Hosiery.

   Where are you?

   _____

2. Go to the back of the store. Take the elevator to the basement. It's across from the elevator, straight ahead.

   Where are you?

   _____

3. Take the elevator to the second floor. Turn left and go to Men's Outerwear. Turn right. Go straight. It's between the Men's Shoes and the Men's Sleepwear departments.

   Where are you?

   _____

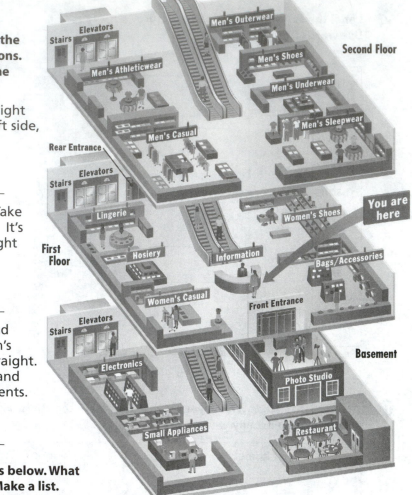

13 Choose one of the travel destinations below. What clothing will you pack for the trip? Make a list. Include any shoes, outerwear, casual, formal, or wild clothes you will need.

Go skiing in the Swiss Alps.

Hear gospel music at a Harlem church in New York City, USA.

Go dancing at a nightclub in Paris, France.

Go swimming on Boracay Island, Philippines.

GRAMMAR
BOOSTER

A ▷ **Complete the sentences with words from the box. Use the comparative form.**

| comfortable | expensive | fast | large | healthful | warm | old | ~~short~~ |

1. Women are usually _shorter than_ men.

2. A coat is _____ a sweater.

3. Cars are _____ radios.

4. Your grandmother is _____ your nephew.

5. Russia is _____ Spain.

6. Airplanes are _____ boats.

7. Sweatpants are _____ suits.

8. Fruit is _____ junk food.

B ▷ **WHAT ABOUT YOU? Answer the questions in complete sentences. Use your own words.**

1. "Who is taller, you or your best friend?"

   (YOU) _____.

2. "Who is bigger, your father or your mother?"

   (YOU) _____.

3. "Which building is bigger, your home or your school?"

   (YOU) _____.

4. "Which language is easier to learn, your native language or English?"

   (YOU) _____.

5. "Which is more fun, playing golf or going dancing?"

   (YOU) _____.

C ▷ **Write questions. Use object pronouns and the words in parentheses.**

1. **A:** I take my mother to the same restaurant every week.

   B: _Where do you take her_ ? (where)

2. **A:** She washes her car a lot.

   B: _____? (when)

3. **A:** He eats fish.

   B: _____? (how often)

4. **A:** My teacher invites her students to her house.

   B: _____? (why)

5. **A:** Monica meets her boyfriend every morning.

   B: _____? (what time)

D Write sentences in two ways using the words indicated. Add prepositions if necessary.

1. the address / give / her

   Give her the address   .   _Give the address to her_   .

2. Tina / gifts / him / buys

   _____.   _____.

3. the teacher / homework / us / gives

   _____.   _____.

4. the waiters / them / food / serve

   _____.   _____.

JUST FOR **FUN**

Look at the pictures. Find the names of the items of clothing in the puzzle.
Circle the ten words. Words can be across (→) or down (↓).

s	w	e	a	b	o	x	e	r	s	o	s
l	p	n	t	a	s	o	k	n	o	s	w
b	e	i	s	g	n	a	g	r	c	a	e
o	m	g	h	x	t	i	s	t	k	o	a
x	i	h	p	a	j	a	m	a	s	b	t
y	n	t	w	i	n	r	b	r	z	e	p
t	i	g	h	t	s	u	o	u	p	a	a
s	h	o	r	t	s	n	x	n	a	n	n
b	a	w	z	o	p	a	l	b	e	l	t
w	i	n	d	b	r	e	a	k	e	r	s

A Riddle for You!

Riddle: Mr. and Mrs. Bigger had a baby. Which one is the biggest?

Answer: The baby. He's a little Bigger.

Getting Away

TOPIC PREVIEW

1 Match the vacation words on the left with their meanings on the right.
Write the letter on the line.

1. ____ wildlife
2. ____ accommodations
3. ____ beverages
4. ____ entertainment
5. ____ meals
6. ____ cruise
7. ____ rates

a. travel by ship or boat
b. drinks
c. movies, concerts, plays
d. food
e. hotels, hostels, resorts
f. animals
g. the money you pay

2 WHAT ABOUT YOU? In your country, where would you go on vacation for . . .

nature and wildlife?	history and culture?
family activities?	physical activities?

3 WHAT ABOUT YOU? Complete the paragraph. Use your <u>own</u> ideas.

When I go on vacation, I usually go to _____.
I like to visit _____ and see _____.
I like to eat _____. I don't really like to _____.

LESSON 1

4 ▸ **Complete the conversations. Write the best response on the lines. Use sentences from the box.**

| No, thanks. | That's too bad. | Pretty boring. | Well, that's good. | No, not too bad. |

Need help with your things?

1. _____

So how was the trip?

2. _____

I'll bet the food was terrible.

3. _____

Of course, the train wasn't on time.

4. _____

But it was very scenic.

5. _____

5 Write statements. Use the words in parentheses and <u>was</u>, <u>were</u>, <u>wasn't</u>, or <u>weren't</u>.

1. (The cruise / terrific) _The cruise was terrific_____.

2. (The accommodations / pretty nice) _____.

3. (Our room / a little small) _____.

4. (There / not / any good family activities) _____.

5. (There / a lot of friendly people) _____.

6. (The flight / not / very long) _____.

6 Write <u>yes</u> / <u>no</u> questions and short answers. Use the past tense of <u>be</u>.

1. **A:** (your / bus / on time) _Was your bus on time_____?
   B: No, _it wasn't_____. It was over an hour late!

2. **A:** (the movie theater / open) _____?
   B: Yes, _____. They had a late show.

3. **A:** (the weather / good) _____?
   B: No, _____. It rained every day.

4. **A:** (there / a movie / on your flight) _____?
   B: No, _____. It was so boring!

5. **A:** (there / any problems / at the airport) _____?
   B: Yes, _____. My flight was canceled.

7 Complete the conversation with information questions. Use the past tense of <u>be</u>.

A: Hey, Marty. _____?
1. Where / you / last weekend

B: My wife and I took a little vacation.

A: Really? _____?
2. How / it

B: Too short! But we stayed at a great resort.

A: Oh yeah? _____?
3. Where / the resort

B: Over in Wroxton. We drove down Friday night.

A: Wroxton? That's pretty far.

_____?
4. How long / the drive

B: About three-and-a-half hours. There wasn't any traffic.

A: Nice! _____?
5. And / how / the weather

B: Actually, the weather was pretty good.
   Only rained once!

A: Sounds wonderful.

_____?
6. How long / you / there

B: Just three days. We didn't want to come home!

8 ▸ **WHAT ABOUT YOU?** Read the questions. Write responses. Use your <u>own</u> words.

1. "When was your last vacation?"

   YOU _____

   _____.

2. "How long was it?"

   YOU _____

   _____.

3. "How was the weather?"

   YOU _____

   _____.

MOST POPULAR VACATION

According to the World Tourism Organization, the world's most popular vacation destination is France. In 2001, 76.5 million international visitors came to France. That was 11% of all international travelers! It was also more than the population of France, which was around 60 million. Spain was second, with 49.5 million visitors, and the U.S. was in third place, with 45.5 million.

SOURCE: www.guinnessworldrecords.com

LESSON 2

9 ▸ Complete the chart with the present or the simple past tense.

	Present tense	Simple past tense
1.	call	
2.		arrived
3.		studied
4.	get	
5.	stop	

	Present tense	Simple past tense
6.		went
7.	buy	
8.	do	
9.	leave	
10.		ate

10 ▸ Choose the correct responses to complete the conversation. Write the letter on the line.

A: Hi, Emily. I didn't see you at the gym this weekend.

B: ___
   1.

A: Really? How was it?

B: ___
   2.

A: What did you do?

B: ___
   3.

A: That sounds nice. Did the kids have a good time?

B: ___
   4.

a. We went to the zoo and ate lunch downtown.

b. Yes, they did. They love nature and wildlife. And they slept all the way home in the car!

c. I didn't go. We took the kids to Toronto.

d. Terrific. We had a lot of fun.

11 **Complete the sentences with the simple past tense.**

1. I _____ some nice souvenirs, but I
   (buy)

   _____ a lot of money.
   (not spend)

2. We _____ to Montreal, but we _____
   (fly)   (take)

   the train back.

3. We _____ a great time at the baseball
   (have)

   game! The kids _____ sandwiches and
   (eat)

   _____ soda, and they _____ the
   (drink)   (watch)

   game, too—a little!

4. I _____ at 10:00. I _____
   (leave)   (get)

   back at noon.

12 **Read the responses. Put the words in order to make questions.**

1. **A:** (did / eat / Where / you) _Where did you eat_ _____?

   B: At a Japanese restaurant.

2. **A:** (Did / go / with Jane / you) _____?

   B: No, I went with Deanna.

3. **A:** (like / Did / the art exhibit / you) _____?

   B: No, I didn't. It was pretty boring.

4. **A:** (you / did / When / leave) _____?

   B: We left on Tuesday morning.

5. **A:** (What / she / buy / did) _____?

   B: She bought a souvenir T-shirt.

6. **A:** (did / play tennis / Where / you) _____?

   B: At the resort.

7. **A:** (did / How long / stay / you) _____?

   B: A little over a month.

13 **WHAT ABOUT YOU?** **Read the questions. Write a response. Use your <u>own</u> words.**

1. "Did you sleep late this morning?"

   (YOU) _____.

2. "Where did you eat lunch yesterday?"

   (YOU) _____.

3. "When did you exercise this week?"

   (YOU) _____.

14 Look at the vacation picture.

Now read the statements. Who is speaking? Match each statement to a person in the picture. Write the letter on the line.

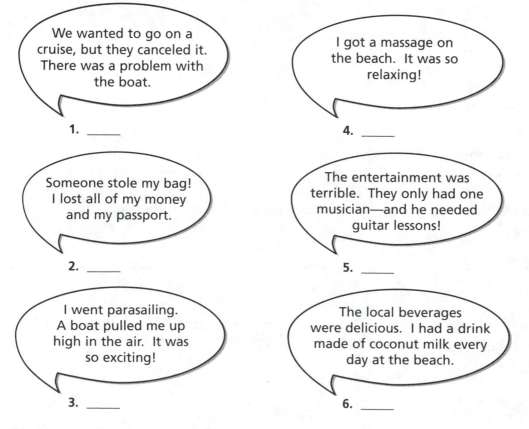

We wanted to go on a cruise, but they canceled it. There was a problem with the boat.

1. _____

I got a massage on the beach. It was so relaxing!

4. _____

Someone stole my bag! I lost all of my money and my passport.

2. _____

The entertainment was terrible. They only had one musician—and he needed guitar lessons!

5. _____

I went parasailing. A boat pulled me up high in the air. It was so exciting!

3. _____

The local beverages were delicious. I had a drink made of coconut milk every day at the beach.

6. _____

15 **Complete the vacation postcard. Use adjectives from the box.**

| scary | relaxing | perfect | terrible | scenic | unusual |

Dear Hank,

Hawaii is incredible! I arrived yesterday, and the view of the white beach from the airplane was very (1) _____. Today the weather was (2) _____ —not too hot with a beautiful blue sky. This morning a woman gave me a soothing massage right on the beach. Wow! It was so (3) _____ that I fell asleep! After that, I tried something new and different—a beverage served in a coconut! The coconut milk tasted a little (4) _____, but it was pretty good. Not everything is perfect, though. After lunch I went parasailing. A boat pulled me high up into the air. I don't like high places! It was really (5) _____. And the entertainment is (6) _____! This afternoon, a musician played Hawaiian guitar music. I'm not a big Hawaiian music fan! Well, that's all for now. Wish you were here!

Love, Laura

Hank Williams
28 Hillis Terrace
Madison, WI 53704

GRAMMAR BOOSTER

A Choose the correct response. Write the letter on the line.

1. ____ "How was your vacation?"
2. ____ "Where did you go?"
3. ____ "How long were you there?"
4. ____ "Was the weather good?"
5. ____ "How were the accommodations?"
6. ____ "Were there a lot of things to do?"
7. ____ "Was the food OK?"

a. No, it wasn't. It rained all week.
b. Terrific. It was so much fun.
c. Jamaica.
d. Yes, there were. We were busy all the time.
e. Yes, it was good. But a little spicy.
f. Just a week.
g. Clean and comfortable.

B Correct the errors in the e-mail message.

Dear Mari,

                        was
My vacation ~~were~~ lots of fun! My family and I went to Hawaii. The only

problem were the hotel. It was very nice. The beds were terrible.

Everything else were perfect. There was many activities. My favorite

activity wasn't parasailing. It were terrific.

Laura

C **WHAT ABOUT YOU?** Write questions with the past tense of <u>be</u>. Then answer the questions with complete sentences. Use your <u>own</u> words.

1. when / your last vacation _____?

    (YOU) _____.

2. it / long _____?

    (YOU) _____.

3. how / the hotel _____?

    (YOU) _____.

4. the weather / good _____?

    (YOU) _____.

5. how many / people / with you _____?

    (YOU) _____.

D ▸ **Rewrite the sentences. Use the simple past tense and a past time expression.**

1. We go to the beach every year.

   _We went to the beach last year_____.

2. The weather isn't very good today.

   _____.

3. How long does the trip usually take?

   _____?

4. We don't stay in a hotel.

   _____.

5. I often cook clams at the beach.

   _____.

6. Everyone has a good time.

   _____.

7. Is your flight canceled?

   _____?

E ▸ **Read the statements. Write questions in response using the words in parentheses.**

1. **A:** She bought a new printer.

   B: _Why did she buy a new printer_____? (why)

2. **A:** We went on vacation.

   B: _____? (where)

3. **A:** They went to the gym.

   B: _____? (when)

4. **A:** I visited some friends.

   B: _____? (who)

5. **A:** He spent a lot of money.

   B: _____? (how much)

JUST FOR **FUN**

1 ▸ Find the words in the puzzle. Circle the words. Words can be across (→) or down (↓).

scenic

amazing

relaxing

interesting

boring

bumpy

unusual

short

comfortable

long

exciting

incredible

l	v	s	c	e	n	i	c	b	c	s	q	a
k	m	w	q	o	x	l	q	g	o	v	b	l
l	h	n	b	e	k	o	w	x	m	c	g	s
r	e	l	a	x	i	n	g	q	f	d	q	x
l	p	o	e	c	p	g	r	e	o	f	g	k
q	g	d	f	i	x	l	f	m	r	t	i	l
s	s	i	n	t	e	r	e	s	t	i	n	g
t	h	x	d	i	n	t	t	b	a	g	c	m
b	o	r	i	n	g	v	y	u	b	s	r	y
u	r	c	c	g	b	c	k	l	l	m	e	c
m	t	b	q	l	j	y	o	p	e	v	d	l
p	p	a	m	a	z	i	n	g	h	r	i	g
y	m	j	l	p	a	m	a	s	y	v	b	o
v	a	y	d	b	u	n	u	s	u	a	l	l
b	x	f	k	t	x	l	h	u	a	f	e	y

2 ▸ What can you do in your free time? Unscramble the underlined words. Write the activity on the line.

1. visit the <u>ozo</u>   = _visit the zoo_____

2. see a <u>labbasel meag</u> = _____

3. visit an <u>tar semumu</u> = _____

4. do <u>bacseori</u>   = _____

5. play <u>fgol</u>   = _____

6. take a <u>ruisce</u>   = _____

7. go on a <u>rasfai</u>   = _____

The food was terrible—
and the portions were
too small!

A Joke for You!

Taking Transportation

TOPIC PREVIEW

1 Look at the departure schedule and the clock. Read the statements. Check ✔ true or false.

	true	false
1. The next flight to Porto Alegre is at 5:50 p.m.	☐	☐
2. Flight 902 to São Luis is leaving from Gate G4.	☐	☐
3. The flight to Caracas is delayed.	☐	☐
4. Flight number 267 is going to Belo Horizonte.	☐	☐
5. Passengers on Flight 56 are taking Asiana Airline.	☐	☐
6. Flight 60 is late.	☐	☐

RAPID AIR BRASILIA DEPARTURES

Destination	FLT/No.	Departs	Gate	Status
São Paulo	56	15:50	G4	departed
Belo Horizonte	267	16:10	G3	boarding
Rio de Janeiro	89	16:10	G9	boarding
São Paulo	58	16:50	G4	now 17:25
São Luis	902	17:00	G3	on time
São Paulo	60	17:50	G4	delayed
Porto Alegre	763	17:50	G3	on time
Caracas	04	18:05	G1	canceled
Rio de Janeiro	91	18:10	G9	on time
São Paulo	62	18:50	G4	on time

`15:50`

2 Choose the correct response. Write the letter on the line.

1. _____ "Oh, no! The train's leaving in four minutes."
2. _____ "I took Northern Airlines to Hong Kong."
3. _____ "I'm looking for the departure gate."
4. _____ "Are you taking the 8:30 train?"
5. _____ "How often do you fly?"

a. Really? How was the flight?

b. Once or twice a year.

c. Yes, I am. You too?

d. Which one?

e. We should hurry!

3 Put the conversation in order. Write the number on the line.

_1_ Can I help you?

___ Let's see. The local leaves from track 23, lower level.

___ That sounds OK. What's the track number?

___ Oh, no! What should I do?

___ Yes. Can I still make the 10:05 express train to Antwerp?

___ Sorry, you missed it.

___ Well, you could take a local train. There's one at 11:05.

___ Thanks very much.

4 **Choose the correct response. Circle the letter.**

1. "I missed the 7:30. What should I do?"
   a. No, I'm sorry.   b. You could take the 9:10.   c. It left five minutes ago.

2. "The next bus is at 5:50."
   a. Is it an express?   b. Is it a direct flight?   c. One way or round trip?

3. "One way or round trip?"
   a. Two tickets, please.   b. Yes, please.   c. One way.

4. "Oh, no! The train is leaving in three minutes!"
   a. No, I'm sorry.   b. No, you couldn't.   c. We should hurry!

5 **Read the article. Choose the correct answer.**

Traveling by Bullet

The Japanese Shinkansen, or "bullet trains," began service in 1964. They carried passengers between Tokyo and Osaka. The first trains traveled at 210 km per hour. Today, shinkansen trains on Japan's main island of Honshu connect Tokyo with most of the larger cities. They travel at speeds between 240 and 300 km per hour. In 2007, the Japanese Railway is going to introduce a 350 km-per-hour train. One tip for bullet train travelers: Get to your departure gate on time. Shinkansen trains are almost never late. In 1999, the average lateness per train was twenty-four seconds!

SOURCE: www.jrtr.net

1. A shinkansen is
   a. a city in Japan.
   b. a train station.
   c. a fast Japanese train.

2. Japanese bullet trains are
   a. always late.
   b. almost always on time.
   c. often canceled.

6 **Complete each sentence or question. Use <u>could</u> or <u>should</u> and the base form of the verb.**

1. Want my advice? _____ the express. _____ the local, but it takes
   You / take   You / take
   thirty minutes longer.

2. _____! _____ the 7:30!
   You / hurry   You / make

3. _____ round-trip tickets. They are cheaper than two one-way tickets, and she
   She / buy
   won't have to wait in another ticket line.

4. _____ an aisle seat in the rear of the plane or a window seat in the front.
   We / take
   What do you think? What seats _____?
   we / take

5. The flight is delayed. _____ late for the meeting. _____ the office?
   We / be   we / call

6. No, _____ a direct flight. They tried, but all the flights had a stop in Anchorage.
   they / not / get

7 Look at the schedules. Which train should the people take? Write your advice on the line.

Metropolitan Railroad			
	Local	Express	Local
White Plains	7:25	8:22	9:05
Scarsdale	7:42	-	9:22
Bronxville	8:05	-	9:40
Harlem 125th St.	8:24	-	9:59
Grand Central Terminal	8:30	8:59	10:06

I live in White Plains. I need a train that will arrive in New York City around 9:00 a.m. Could I take the 8:22 express?

1. _Yes, you could take_ _the 8:22_ ____.

I live in White Plains. I'm meeting my boss at Grand Central Station at 8:45 a.m. We're going to an important meeting and I can't be late. Which train should I take?

2. _____ _____ _____.

I live in Scarsdale. I've got some free time tomorrow morning. I need to go shopping for a new laptop in New York City. Most computer stores open at 10:00 a.m. What time should I be at the Scarsdale train station?

3. _____ _____ _____.

I'm in White Plains. I want to go to Bronxville. Could I take an express train or should I take a local?

4. _____ _____ _____.

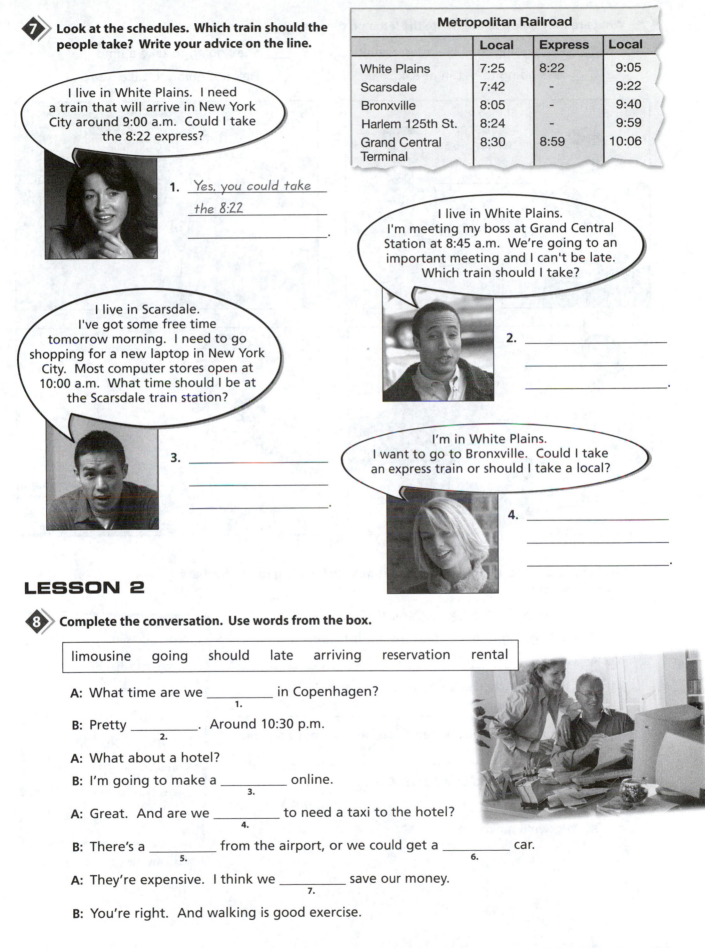

LESSON 2

8 Complete the conversation. Use words from the box.

| limousine going should late arriving reservation rental |

A: What time are we _____ in Copenhagen?
1.

B: Pretty _____. Around 10:30 p.m.
2.

A: What about a hotel?

B: I'm going to make a _____ online.
3.

A: Great. And are we _____ to need a taxi to the hotel?
4.

B: There's a _____ from the airport, or we could get a _____ car.
5. 6.

A: They're expensive. I think we _____ save our money.
7.

B: You're right. And walking is good exercise.

9 ► **What are they going to do? Write the letter on the line.**

1. ____ She's going to make a reservation.   3. ____ She's going to take a limo.

2. ____ He's going to get in at 8:45.   4. ____ He's not going to take a taxi.

10 ► **Read the responses. Complete each question with be going to and the base form of the verb.**

1. **A:** Where _is Paul going to meet us_ _____?

   B: Paul's going to meet us at the airport café.

2. **A:** Who _____?

   B: I think Gretchen is going to buy the tickets.

3. **A:** When _____?

   B: I'm going to need the rental car on Thursday and Friday.

4. **A:** What time _____?

   B: They're going to arrive at 5:50 p.m.

5. **A:** _____ our 6:20 flight?

   B: Yes, we'll make it.

> The world's longest direct run train (without changing trains) is 10,214 km, from Moscow, Russia, to Pyongyang, North Korea. One train a week takes this route. The trip takes almost eight days!

SOURCE: www.guinnessworldrecords.com

11 **WHAT ABOUT YOU?** **What are your plans for today? Complete the chart. Put a check ☑ in the box.**

	I did this.	I'm going to do this.	I'm not going to do this.
call a friend			
check my e-mail			
go shopping			
clean my house			
cook			
study			
exercise			
take a taxi			
other . . .			

12 **Now write sentences about your plans for today. Use the future tense with be going to.**

I'm going to call a friend tonight after work.

LESSONS 3 AND 4

13 **Who is speaking? Write a gate agent or a passenger on the line.**

Good afternoon, ladies and gentlemen. Flight 58 has been delayed. The new departure time is 7:00.

1. _a gate agent_

We got bumped from our flight. What should we do?

2. _____

We are now boarding first class passengers for Asiana Flight 58. Please have your boarding passes ready.

3. _____

a gate agent

a passenger

The flight is overbooked. I think I'm going to volunteer to take a later flight.

4. _____

Can I still make the 6:45 flight to São Paulo?

5. _____

This is a gate change for Asiana Airlines, Flight 58, with service to Tokyo, Japan. The new gate is Gate 8G.

6. _____

14 Look at the pictures. Match each statement with the correct picture.

1. ____ Our flight was canceled. The airplane had mechanical problems.

2. ____ The cruise was terrible. My whole family got seasick!

3. ____ Sorry we're late. We missed the express train and had to take a local.

4. ____ My dad had to wait over an hour to get through security.

5. ____ We had an accident. Our sightseeing bus hit a tree.

15 Look at the pictures of Joe Cooney's trip. Then read the statements.
Check ✔ <u>true</u> or <u>false</u>.

	true	false
1. His flight was on time.	☐	☐
2. He sat in an aisle seat.	☐	☐
3. His plane had mechanical problems.	☐	☐
4. He missed the hotel shuttle bus.	☐	☐
5. He drove a rental car to the hotel.	☐	☐

16 Write a short paragraph about Joe Cooney's trip.

GRAMMAR BOOSTER

A ▶ **Read the questions and statements. Correct the mistakes.**

1. You should ~~to go~~ *go to* track 57.

2. Where could he to get a train to Hampstead?

3. Bette can't takes a flight to Tokyo.

4. When we could leave?

5. How late can he to board?

6. He shoulds choose an aisle seat.

B ▶ **Read the questions. Complete the responses.**

1. **A:** Should she buy a one-way ticket?

   B: No, _she shouldn't_____. It's more expensive.

2. **A:** Can he bring food on the flight?

   B: Yes, _____.

3. **A:** Could I take the number 3 train?

   B: Yes, _____. It will take you to the right station.

4. **A:** Can we get seats together?

   B: No, _____. I'm sorry. We only have a few seats left.

5. **A:** Should they get a rental car?

   B: Yes, _____. It is more convenient.

C ▶ **Rewrite the sentences to express future actions. Use be going to and the base form of the verb.**

1. She studied for three hours.

   _She's going to study for three hours_____ tomorrow.

2. They ran two miles last Sunday.

   _____ next Sunday.

3. We had a party last week.

   _____ next week.

4. I went to school yesterday.

   _____ tomorrow.

5. You did a great job.

   _____.

JUST FOR FUN

1 ▶ **Look at the sentences. Write the words. Then look at the gray boxes ▢.**

1. The plane is full. I'm going to ____ to be bumped.

2. We were late because the plane had mechanical ____.

3. The agent at the gate needs to see your ____ pass.

4. I'm going to have to cancel my hotel ____.

5. We should hurry. There's always a line at the ____ gate.

6. I don't have to take the early train, but I ____.

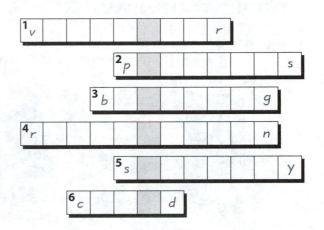

1 v | | | | | ▓ | | r
2 p | | | | | ▓ | | | s
3 b | | | | ▓ | | g
4 r | | | | | ▓ | | | n
5 s | | | | ▓ | | y
6 c | | ▓ | d

What's the new word? _____

2 ▶ **Read the poem. Can you solve the riddle?**

As I was going to St. Ives
by Mother Goose*

As I was going to St. Ives,

I met a man with seven wives;

Every wife had seven sacks,

Every sack had seven cats,

Every cat had seven kits;

Kits, cats, sacks, and wives,

How many were going to St. Ives?

*"Mother Goose" rhymes are traditional English poems for children. No one knows who wrote them.

Answer: One.

Shopping Smart

TOPIC PREVIEW

1 How do you use an ATM machine? Look at the pictures on the left. Match each picture with an instruction on the right.

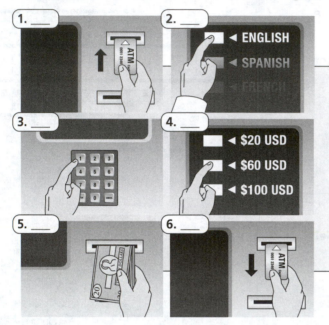

1. ___
2. ___
   ◄ ENGLISH
   ◄ SPANISH
   ◄ FRENCH
3. ___
4. ___
   ◄ $20 USD
   ◄ $60 USD
   ◄ $100 USD
5. ___
6. ___

a. Take your ATM card.

b. Enter the amount of cash you want.

c. Take your cash.

d. Put your ATM card in the card slot.

e. Choose your language.

f. Enter your Personal Identification Number (PIN).

2 WHAT ABOUT YOU? Look at the list on the left. In your <u>own</u> country, what could people use to pay for these things? Check ☑ the boxes.

	Cash	Credit Card	Traveler's Check
dinner at a restaurant	☐	☐	☐
a newspaper from a newsstand	☐	☐	☐
an airplane ticket	☐	☐	☐
a CD from an online music store	☐	☐	☐
a snack in a convenience store	☐	☐	☐
a hotel room	☐	☐	☐

LESSON 1

3 Choose the correct response. Circle the letter.

1. "I'm looking for an MP3 player for my son."
   a. You think so?   b. What about this one?   c. It's the best.

2. "How much did you want to spend?"
   a. I wanted $100.   b. No more than $100.   c. I spent $100.

3. "We have two or three in your price range."
   a. It can't hurt to ask.   b. Could I have a look?   c. Good idea.

4. "Why do you recommend Diego brand DVD players?"
   a. They're the easiest to use.   b. They're the least popular.   c. They're the worst.

4 **Complete the conversation. Write the letter on the line.**

A: Excuse me. I'd like to buy a camcorder.

B: _____
　　1.

A: I don't know. What do you recommend?

B: _____
　　2.

A: Actually, that's a little out of my price range.

B: _____
　　3.

A: Is it difficult to use?

B: _____
　　4.

A: OK. Do you accept traveler's checks?

B: _____
　　5.

a. The Power X. It's the most popular.

b. No. And the sound is great.

c. OK. Which one are you interested in?

d. Yes. No problem.

e. The X23 isn't bad, and it's much cheaper.

5 **Look at the chart from a digital camera buying guide.**

COMPARE DIGITAL CAMERAS

Brand / Model	Price	Ease of Use	Size	Weight
Diego Mini 3000	US$239	●●	c	35 g (1.2 oz)
Honshu B100	US$209	●●●	p	283 g (9.9 oz)
Honshu X24	US$139	●	s	180 g (6.3 oz)
Prego 5	US$299	●●●●	s	135 g (4.7 oz)
Vision 2.0	US$449	●●●	s	224 g (7.9 oz)

KEY

●●●●	very easy
●●●	pretty easy
●●	a little difficult
●	difficult
c	compact (small size, can fit in a shirt pocket)
s	standard (medium size, similar to a point and shoot camera)
p	professional (large size, similar to a 35mm camera)

Now write questions with <u>Which</u>. Use the superlative form of the adjectives from the box. Not all adjectives will be used.

~~expensive~~　light　portable　easy to use　cheap　heavy　difficult to use

1. A: _Which camera is the most expensive_ ?

   B: The Vision 2.0.

2. A: _____ ?

   B: The Honshu X24.

3. A: _____ ?

   B: The Diego Mini 3000.

4. A: _____ ?

   B: The Prego 5.

5. A: _____ ?

   B: The Honshu B100.

6 Read each person's statements. For each shopper, recommend a digital camera from the buying guide in Exercise 5. Give a reason for your advice.

"I need a new camera. The one I have now is too heavy. I really want a camera that I can carry in my jacket pocket."

1. (YOU) _____.

"I'm looking for a digital camera for my mother. She isn't good with electronics, so it must be very easy to use. What do you recommend?"

2. (YOU) _____.

"I'd like to have a look at your least expensive digital camera. I can't spend more than $150. Do you have anything in my price range?"

3. (YOU) _____.

LESSON 2

7 Complete the conversations. Use words from the box.

give	fair	too	much
about	more	bowl	enough

A: This _____ is gorgeous. I'd love to get
    1.
it for my sister.

B: It's nice. And it's small _____ to take in your suitcase.
    2.

A: I'm going to ask about the price. I hope it's not
_____ expensive.
3.

A: I'm interested in this bowl. How _____ do you
    4.
want for it?

C: This one is $45.

A: That's a bit _____ than I want to spend.
    5.
I could _____ you $30.
    6.

C: How _____ $35? That's a bargain.
    7.

A: OK. That sounds _____.
    8.

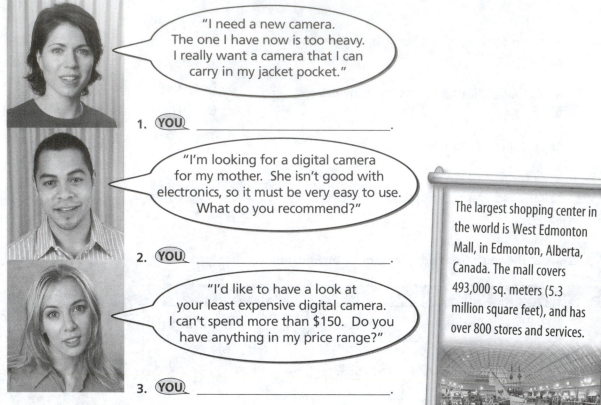

The largest shopping center in the world is West Edmonton Mall, in Edmonton, Alberta, Canada. The mall covers 493,000 sq. meters (5.3 million square feet), and has over 800 stores and services.

The mall complex includes the world's largest indoor amusement park and the world's largest indoor lake. More than 23,000 people work there. And the mall has one more superlative—the world's largest parking lot!

What's the largest shopping center in your city or town?

_____

SOURCE: www.westedmall.com

8 ▶ Complete the sentences. Use <u>too</u> or <u>enough</u> and the adjective in parentheses.

1. I'm not going to read that book. It's _____.
   (boring)

2. Sylvia shouldn't travel alone. She isn't _____.
   (old)

3. I don't want to buy anything in that shop. The people were _____.
   (unfriendly)

4. Tania likes the red rug, but it's _____ for her living room.
   (big)

5. I love this belt, but it isn't _____. I need a size 34.
   (long)

6. Are your shoes _____? We're going to do a lot of walking.
   (comfortable)

7. We wanted to bargain for a lower price, but it was _____.
   (difficult)

LESSONS 3 AND 4

9 ▶ Choose the correct response. Write the response on the line.

1. **A:** $650! I paid $329 for the same camcorder yesterday!

   B: _____

2. **A:** How much do you want for this vase?

   B: _____

3. **A:** You could try to get a better price.

   B: _____

4. **A:** I saved a lot of money on this DVD player. It was only $79.

   B: _____

5. **A:** Here you are, sir. The Atlas Hotel. That's $8.50.

   B: _____

You think so?

What a rip-off!

Thanks. Keep the change.

What a good deal!

The tall one?

10 ▶ Read the statements and questions. Who would probably say this? Check ✔ the boxes.

	Buyer	Seller
1. "All of our scanners are on sale."	☐	☐
2. "I'm almost out of cash."	☐	☐
3. "That's out of my price range."	☐	☐
4. "Wow! What a great deal!"	☐	☐
5. "How about this one? It's our most popular brand."	☐	☐
6. "Can you give me a better price?"	☐	☐

Read the article about bargaining customs around the world. Then read the statements. Check ☑ <u>true</u> or <u>false</u>.

Can you give me a better price?
Bargaining Customs Around the World

Bargaining customs are very different around the world. Few tourists would go shopping in another country without knowing the exchange rate. However, many travelers don't learn anything about the local shopping customs of the place they are visiting before spending money. Understanding when it's OK to bargain can save you a lot of money and make your shopping experience much more enjoyable.

In some countries, bargaining is an important part of the shopping culture. In others, bargaining is not done at all. Here's a bargaining guide for some countries around the world:

Morocco: Bargaining is always expected in the shopping markets. Here bargaining is more than just getting the best price. If you go into a shop and agree to the first price a seller offers, the seller may not be happy. For Moroccans, bargaining is a form of entertainment; it's a game of skill, a little bit of acting, and it's a chance to chat about the weather, business, and family. So be sure to have fun and try to get a better price!

Switzerland: Bargaining is not the custom here. Shop clerks can almost never give you a lower price. However, some hotels may give you a lower rate during the less popular times of year. It can't hurt to ask.

Tahiti: Bargaining is not appropriate in the South Pacific. In fact, it is considered disrespectful to ask for a better price. In the food markets, sellers will even take their fruits and vegetables back home with them, rather than give a discount!

SOURCE: "Lonely Planet Travel Guides"

	true	false
1. Bargaining customs are similar around the world.	☐	☐
2. Generally, market sellers in Morocco love to bargain.	☐	☐
3. In Switzerland, it's OK to bargain for a cheaper hotel room.	☐	☐
4. It can't hurt to ask a fruit seller in Tahiti for a lower price.	☐	☐

WHAT ABOUT YOU? **Write a short paragraph about bargaining in your <u>own</u> country. What items do people bargain for? What items do people never bargain for?**

GRAMMAR BOOSTER

A ▸ Complete the chart.

	Adjective	Comparative form	Superlative form
1.	beautiful		
2.			the most intelligent
3.	big		
4.		more convenient	
5.	busy		
6.			the fastest
7.		safer	
8.	noisy		

B ▸ Complete the conversations with the comparative or the superlative form of the adjective in parentheses.

1. **A:** Which one of these three sweaters do you think is _the prettiest_ (pretty)?

   B: The blue one. The other two are not attractive at all.

2. **A:** How do you like the book?

   B: I don't like it. It's _____ (bad) than the one I read yesterday.

3. **A:** Did you enjoy Australia?

   B: Yes. I think it's one of _____ (interesting) places in the world.

4. **A:** Who is _____ (good) at baseball, you or your brother?

   B: Well, I'm a _____ (fast) base runner, but my brother is a _____ (powerful) hitter. Actually, my dad is the _____ (good) player in the family. He was a star player in college.

5. **A:** Which laptop is _____ (popular)?

   B: Well, the X102 is the _____ (cheap) model in the store. But I actually recommend the X200. It's a little _____ (expensive) than the X102, but much _____ (light).

C ▸ Answer the questions. Use **too** or **enough** and the adjective in parentheses.

1. **A:** Why didn't you buy the camcorder?

   B: (expensive) _It was too expensive_. I need to save money this month.

2. **A:** Is the food too spicy?

   B: (spicy) _____. I'm going to ask for more hot sauce!

3. **A:** What's wrong with these shoes?

   B: I can't wear them. (uncomfortable) _____.

4. **A:** Why don't you like the apartment?

   B: (noisy) _____. I'm looking for a quiet neighborhood.

5. **A:** Why don't you take the train instead of flying?

   B: (fast) _____. I have to get there as soon as possible.

6. **A:** Do you want to go to a jazz concert?

   B: Thanks for asking, but I'm not a jazz music fan. (boring) _____.

1 ▷ **Complete the crossword puzzle.**

Across

1. opposite of best

2. opposite of most

3. the amount something costs

4. ask for a better price

Down

5. pay money

6. a low price; a great ___

7. money you give a waiter or driver

8. money you can pay; your price ___

9. help you get in a restaurant or hotel

2 ▷ **Which words go together? Circle the adjectives with <u>opposite</u> meanings.**

1. (old)	healthy	big	(new)
2. comfortable	large	sweet	small
3. gorgeous	difficult	easy	loose
4. interesting	pretty	fatty	boring
5. expensive	hot	cheap	wild
6. different	similar	nice	formal
7. light	flattering	heavy	unusual
8. liberal	short	portable	long
9. conservative	popular	good	bad